ENCORE LEADERSHIP

*Transforming Time, Talent and Treasure
Into a Legacy that Matters*

ENCORE LEADERSHIP

Transforming Time, Talent and Treasure
Into a Legacy that Matters

Jylla Moore Tearte, PhD

A Comprehensive 12-Step Process and Resource Guide

CRYSTAL STAIRS
PUBLISHERS

Crystal Stairs, Inc., P. O. Box 12215, Atlanta, GA, USA 30355
EncoreLeadership@Crystal-Stairs.com • www.Crystal-Stairs.com

CRYSTAL STAIRS PUBLISHERS

This book includes information from personal experiences and rigorous research. It is intended as a general reference guide. The author and publisher shall have neither liability nor responsibility to anyone with respect to any loss or damage caused, or alleged to be caused, directly or indirectly, by the information contained in this book. Although the author and publisher have made every attempt to ensure accuracy and completeness of information presented, they assume no responsibility for errors, inaccuracies, omissions, or inconsistencies.

A comprehensive resource guide, this book utilizes work from authors who are prolific in their fields as examples for executing the 12-step process discussed in this book. Every attempt has been made to cite the specific work and authors and any oversight is welcome for correction so that proper attribution can be made in future publications.

Cover Design by The Onyx Collection Media Group

ENCORE LEADERSHIP: Transforming Time, Talent and Treasure
Into a Legacy that Matters
By Jylla Moore Tearte, PhD

ISBN (Trade Paperback)   978-0-9722441-4-5
ISBN (Hardcover)   978-0-9722441-2-1
ISBN (Kindle eBook)   978-0-9722441-5-2
ISBN (iPad/Nook eBook)   978-0-9722441-6-9

Library of Congress Control Number: 2013908301

Printed in the United States of America

DEDICATION

I dedicate this book to my family, especially:

My mother and father, Vera and Julius;

My husband, Curtis, and our children, Anjylla, Cherice and David;

Maxine and Lloyd;

Julius and Sylvia; John and Celia;

My mother-in-law, Glendy;

Lillian and Rebecca;

and, Elizabeth and Maurice.

This book is dedicated to the women and men who recognize that their journey in life is not measured by personal accomplishments, but by the joy given to others through their ability to be a vessel for the good of humanity. They are Encore Leaders. The women and men who continuously seek to use their talents to live up to their true identity are Encore Leaders. The women and men who THINK that each day is the best day of the rest of their lives are Encore Leaders. The women and men who help others as a fundamental responsibility for the privilege of living on earth are Encore Leaders. The women and men who thrive on re-imagining and living a world of peaceful solitude inspired by appreciating that to whom much has been given, much is still expected are Encore Leaders. The women and men who always seek to be better than best and greater than great are Encore Leaders. The women and men who rest peacefully at night knowing that the hand they stretched out to others was a life preserve given just when someone needed it most are Encore Leaders.

This book is also dedicated to the men and women who make and have made my Encore Leadership work possible.

I am truly blessed and grateful!

Jylla

Acknowledgments

The people whose names are included in this section have various degrees of closeness to me and to my work. Some of these individuals are close ties in my network and others are tied through the inspirational observation of their work and their example. All of these individuals have influenced my THINKing to the extent that I acknowledge them in this book.

I begin with my college freshman-year English teacher, Mrs. Mattie T. Lakin, who gave me the gift of love of literature; my dissertation committee, Dr. Ram Tenkasi, Dr. Tim Goodly, Dr. Peter Sorensen, and Cohort 6 that challenged my THINKing and my intellect; Dr. Ella Bell who steered me to Benedictine University with Dr. Therese Yaeger and Dr. Jim Ludema; they are a few of the women and men who make my re-invention possible.

Livingstone College Classmates, class of 1976 — we were a mighty class beneath the maples and the oaks. Thanks to each of you for staying connected as we travel this stage of our life's journey together. A special note of thanks to Marie McCleave, network central; my dear roommates, Cora Davis and Tressia Blount; Virginia Woodruff, Bill Scales, and to Bishop Dennis Proctor.

My IBM business colleagues and my Inscape Publishing associates, thanks for influencing my journey. I thank and appreciate the clients who have given Crystal Stairs, Inc. the opportunity to partner in developing their leadership talent. They include: Cardinal Health, AARP, GE, NBC, IBM, Microsoft, CA, Executive Leadership Council, ITSMF, NAWBO, Accenture, EDS, Shell, Wachovia, PepsiCo, Dana, Blockbuster, Unlimited

Results, Cisco, Leadership At Its' Best, Value City Department Stores, Grainger, Fortune Brands, Robinson Group Consulting, Northwestern University, Jackson State University, Savannah State University, RCF, Time Warner, The National Black MBA Association, Thurgood Marshall College Fund, The Chicago Urban League, and the University of Illinois at Urbana-Champaign.

My Sisters of Zeta Phi Beta Sorority, Inc., especially Past Grands Dr. Janice Gantt Kissner *(d)* and Lullelia Walker Harrison *(d)*; Dr. E. Fran Johnson; Regional Directors in my administration – Lady Bessie Canty, Doris M. Stokes, Nathalia M. East Roberts, Laura Farwell, Rosie Thompson-Pridgen, Dr. Rosalind Hale, Dr. Nell Williams Ingram, Norma Collins, Marilyn Brooks, and Lisa Givens; current International President, Mary Breaux Wright, and to all my Zeta Phi Beta Sorority Sisters who never cease to amaze me with their love for serving others and their gift in 1992, which allowed me to lead as the International President. To my Sigma Brothers for always loving me as a sister, in particular, Carter D. Womack, Bill Stanley, Peter Adams, Arthur Thomas, Paul Griffin and Jimmy Hammock.

To the amazing women and men who have given me the opportunity to work with them in strategically THINKing and positioning their teams for success: Bruce Carver, Martin Davis, Cathy Mock, Andrea Zopp, Ava Youngblood, Dee Wood, Peter Campbell, Sheila Talton, Alana Robinson, Marilyn Johnson, Mike Crest, Shelley Hubert, Michael Robinson, Linda Bates Parker *(d)*, Kim Wilson, Wanda McKenzie, Rosalyn Wesley, Dwayne Ashley, Kurt Olson, B. J. Bushur; and my Odyssey Network sisters, Linda Spradley Dunn, Cheryl Walker-Robertson, and Ronda Williams.

To women who are modeling and have modeled the way for so many others: Dr. Westina Matthews, Ester Silva Parker, Jeri DeVard, Dr. Dorothy I. Height *(d)*, Vanessa Weaver, The Honorable Alexis Herman, Johnnie M. Booker, Barbara Ellis, Ingrid Saunders Jones, Tybra Arthur, Ambassador Ertharin Cousin, Shellye Archambeau, First Lady Michelle Obama, Paula Banks, Terrie Williams, Robin Sternbergh, Amy Castaneda, Denise Banasak, Dee Dee Gorgol, Jane Smith, Melba Hill, Eunice Jones Obeng, Esq., Claudia Geocaris, T. Hudson Jordan, Susie Wylie, Kim Sawyer, Deb Elam and Nancy Harding.

To special men who support the efforts of concern to my heart: Ted Childs, Rod Adkins, Don Thompson, Michael Thompson, Mr. Jackson, Charles Brummell, Al Zollar, Ira Hall, Larry Quinlan, Curvie Burton, Doug Ash, Larry Drake, Greg Morrison, Carl Brooks, Will Lucas, Carter Drew, Darwin Davis *(d)*, William Hill, Esq., Lee Walker, Marco McMillian *(d)*, Maurice Arthur, Dwight DeClouette, Marv Dyson, Greg Morris, John Charters, O'Neal Robinson, Larry Hart, Rob Hagans, James Morris, Tim Hart, Greg Wylie, Dwight Kelly, Kevin Christie and Will Saunders.

To the HUES of Hinsdale and Burr Ridge, I thank you for the friendship that transcends all being: Val Reed, Liz Thompson, Dana Perry, Kim Dyson, Debra Morris, Michele Thompson, Shirley Brummell, Audrey Walker *(d)*, and Linda Jackson. To the First Tuesday Ladies Luncheon group in Atlanta, know that I appreciate each of you and enjoy our time together as we celebrate our small corner of the world.

Last, but not least, to the individuals who have touched my life at any point in time and whom I have not specifically listed in this acknowledgment, please know that I appreciate you!

Jylla

Note: (d) Deceased

The Practitioner

A SPECIAL SALUTE TO MR. EARL G. GRAVES, SR.

I have had the privilege of shadowing my corporate life and my entrepreneurial dreams under the tutelage of *Black Enterprise Magazine*. When I first entered the MBA program at Indiana University, I discovered this amazing journal that captured the stories of individuals whom I never knew existed and inscribed them onto the pages of history. These industry movers and shakers were "Black like me," and I was mesmerized with their accomplishments and their success. For me, it was a little girl's dream that had come true when I met Mr. Earl G. Graves, Sr. and was actually featured in a story in the magazine in the March 1997 issue. (Editors, 1997)

I still faithfully read and follow the stories published in the magazine. In January 2012, Mr. Graves, Sr. wrote the thought-provoking editorial, "An Apology to Dr. King" in which he shared that "I know intimately the ultimate sacrifice that King made – based on the promise of future generations – so that we would have the opportunities that we enjoy today. It's a promise we have failed to keep... My generation owes an apology to King for having dropped the baton... Now, it is up to our children and grand-children to continue the fight..."

I hope that my work with Encore Leaders will be worthy of the continued fight!

The Scholar

A SPECIAL SALUTE TO DR. ELLA EDMONDSON BELL

There are no coincidences. This statement is a central concept that speaks to the underpinnings of understanding the transition that one embarks upon. It was no coincidence that I met Dr. Ella Bell on the platform of the train station in Philadelphia as we were both traveling from the National Black MBA Conference to the Congressional Black Caucus Conference in Washington, DC, in September 2006.

We ended up talking the entire trip. As I shared my excitement about the book I had written, *Due North! Strengthen Your Leadership Assets*, Dr. Bell unequivocally challenged the rigor of the research that formulated my determination of assets important to succeed in corporate America. This dialogue led her to the suggestion that I should consider studying in a PhD program at Benedictine University. Not knowing that the university was less than 20 minutes from the home I lived in outside of Chicago, I recognized the intervention of the ordering of my life. And within 120 days, I had been accepted into the next cohort that was to start in April 2007.

My journey into scholarly pursuit had been launched. My dissertation topic emerged. My path had been navigated to explore and to gain scholarly credentials related to transitions. Dr. Bell is acknowledged as the scholar extraordinaire who guided my transition journey as a scholar.

Contents

Acknowledgments vii

The Practitioner.. xi

A Special Salute to Mr. Earl G. Graves, Sr.................................... **xi**

The Scholar xiii

A Special Salute to Dr. Ella Edmondson Bell............................... **xiii**

Prologue..xix

Introduction... **xix**

How this book is structured .... **xxi**

**CRACKING THE TRANSITION CODE
DISSERTATION EXECUTIVE SUMMARY** 1

THE RESEARCH FOUNDATION 3

Overview of the study... 3

Exigency for the study 4

Research Methodology 9

Research Questions 11

Analysis and Findings.. 11

Boundaries and Limitations of the study................................ 13

TRANSITION TIPPING POINTS 15

THE TRANSITION COMPETENCY OPTIMIZATION MODEL©............. 25

Definitions of the Transition Competency Model 28

Sources of the Factors within the Categories 28

Mapping Factors within Categories to Transition Competencies.............. 28

Discussion of the Transition Competencies............................... 30

THE ENCORE LEADERSHIP PROCESS© 37

OVERVIEW 39

The Leadership Maturation Life Cycle© 40

The Transition Tipping Point 43

Transition Tipping Point Vocabulary 44

Encore Leadership Mindset **45**

   1. Having "An Attitude of Gratitude" 45

   2. Striving for Success and Significance 47

   3. Sharing Wisdom 49

   4. Mattering 51

   5. Appreciating Solitude 53

   6. Knowing your "Good Life" 55

   7. Valuing the Freedom to Choose 56

Encore Leadership Community (TGIFiACT) **57**

Poignant, Provocative and Pivotal Questions **59**

THE 4 PHASES AND THE 12 STEPS OF THE
ENCORE LEADERSHIP PROCESS 61

I. RE-EXAMINE **64**

   1. Document Journey 64

   2. Determine Purpose 70

   3. Explore Behavior, Values and Beliefs 78

   4. Confirm Passion 91

   5. Proclaim Vision 92

II. REDEFINE **95**

   6. Design Personal Strategic Plan 95

   7. Inventory Assets 102

   8. Build Network 107

III. REINVEST **117**

   9. Brand Identity 117

   10. Execute 124

IV. REIMAGINE **127**

   11. Evaluate the Journey 127

   12. Innovate and Reinvent 128

GETTING STARTED..**131**

    GETTING STARTED 133

        Encore Leadership Coaching..**133**

            Coachability Index 134

            Selecting a Coach 134

        Accountability Partner **135**

        Resources **136**

            Encore Leadership Workbook 136

            Encore Leadership Dashboard 137

            Encore Leadership Journal 139

            Encore Leadership Assessments 139

            Encore Leadership Apps 140

            Encore Leadership Events 141

            Encore Leadership Seminars for Organizations 141

            Encore Leadership Target Audiences 141

            Encore Leaders Communities of Engagement 142

            Legacy Voices 143

        Stay Connected..**145**

    Epilogue 147

    Appendices 149

        Appendix A: Encore Leadership Glossary 149

        Appendix B: One Page Journal 151

        Appendix C: Samuel's 65 Proven Branding Strategies 152

    Bibliography 155

    Index 163

    About The Author 173

Table of Figures

Figure 1. Exploratory Sequential Mixed Methods Research Design Model 9

Figure 2. Mueller's Change Framework 16

Figure 3. The Transition Competency Optimization Model© 25

Figure 4. Retire and Renew Competency Definitions 26

Figure 5. Reframe and Rewire Competency Definitions 27

Figure 6. Sources of the Factors within the Categories 29

Figure 7. Mapping Factors within categories to Transition Competencies 30

Figure 8. The Encore Leadership Process© 39

Figure 9. Leadership Maturation Life Cycle© 40

Figure 10. 4 Phases of the Encore Leadership Process© 62

Figure 11. 12 Steps of the Encore Leadership Process© 63

Figure 12. Transition Journey Exercise 65

Figure 13. Life Purpose Worksheet 72

Figure 14. The Life Spiral 76

Figure 15. Crystal Stairs Life Compass© 81

Figure 16. Personal Interests, Attitudes and Values 82

Figure 17. Beliefs and Values Diagram 88

Figure 18. Personal Strategic Visioning "Plan" 96

Figure 19. Life Options® Assessment 105

Figure 20. Relationship Circles 110

Figure 21. Clarke's Personal Brand 119

Figure 22. The Comfort Zone 125

Figure 23. The Visible Coaching Process© 134

Figure 24. Encore Leadership Dashboard 138

Figure 25. Encore Leadership Assessments and Transition Competencies 140

Figure 26. Legacy Voices 144

Prologue

INTRODUCTION

Encore Leaders are successful people who are engaged in legacy work that matters!

Transforming your life is not easy. It should not be approached haphazardly. I would suggest that it requires focused energy to explore, with transparency, your past, current, and future life in order to transition to your Encore Leadership life. Thus, this book has evolved into what I would define as a comprehensive 12-step process and resource guide to help successful people shift from successful to significant. This book provides a single source for literature and information, which I consider the most provocative THINKing mechanisms to guide Encore Leaders.

The information is organized into 4 phases and twelve 12 steps to achieve a moment in time when your life is transformed. Recognize up front that this process is iterative. Right when you THINK you have figured it out, a new adventure presents itself, and you repeat the keys to continuously innovate and reinvent your life.

Many books have been written about re-inventing careers. These books tend to focus on re-inventing the period of life that is described in the phases that precede the Encore Leadership phase. The Encore Leader phase of the "Leadership Maturation Life Cycle" has been branded by authors with titles like Halftime, Second Act, The Back Nine, and Reclaiming Your Life. These books have challenged individuals to find their passion and to live it! Many are referenced in this book. However, Encore Leadership provides a unique process derived from the research of transitioned and transitioning professionals who recognize that they are confronting the opportunity of a lifetime. Encore Leaders are shifting their time, talent and treasure into building a legacy that matters!

Most Encore Leaders understand that work alone does not fulfill the mission of "mattering" in life. This book reframes knowledge, stories, and experiences that introduce the poignant language of reinvention so that you can speak it and live it. By accentuating the latent, undiscovered being, it is the desire of this author that personal light bulbs will enlighten the journey that one travels as an Encore Leader. This book creates an opportunity for you to use your gifts, which you have carefully honed with years of practice in professional jobs, organizations, churches, and in other institutions where you have invested your time, talent and treasures.

I believe that many individuals, including myself, often find ourselves just existing, and not optimizing the opportunities that have been presented to us. The talented tenth got so comfortable with the perks of success in corporate life that we developed amnesia from whence we had come. Now, complete with a closet of designer knit clothing, shelves of shoes, signature purses, second homes and vacation homes, and a garage with more than one car, it's time to connect a community of countless Encore Leaders who want to count in countless ways!

The time is analogous to the thought process of Tichy and Devanna when they wrote about the need for transformation leaders in corporations. (Tichy, 1986) Their THINKing led to the thought of transformation of leaders to become Encore Leaders. I reflected on their pattern and adapted their thoughts to Encore Leadership that resulted in this book:

> Change, innovation and entrepreneurship infused into a process that is systematic, with purposeful and organized search for changes, systematic analysis, and the capacity to move resources from areas of lesser to greater productivity with a discipline of a predictable set of steps to become strategically aligned; Recognize need to change, create a new vision and institutionalize the change.

We have the intellect to solve many of the challenges confronting future generations. We must recommit to engage and not allow whatever is keeping us down shackle us from getting up. As Bishop W. Darin Moore shared in his Facebook posting on Easter Monday, 2011, "Jesus got UP so that nothing and no one can ever hold us DOWN! Share in the Resurrection!"

This book is not an end all to offer the best books of all time. Rather, it attempts to provide a framework and tools to document your personal journey that will lead to your life as an Encore Leader. Many books have yet to be written by Encore Leaders who will create, author, and publish their stories.

I have capitalized THINK in this book as a reminder to me of the IBM indoctrination where THINK was prevalent in being and doing. Whether on the steps of buildings or on promotional items, the word was powerful and the expression attracted one's mind like a magnet. As an Encore Leader, it is so important to take time to really THINK about your transformation and to act upon the thoughts. Hopefully, when you read the word THINK in this book, it will cause you to pause and seriously THINK!

As I go through the day and ponder the inevitable, I THINK about what it is that I have been uniquely positioned to give to the world. What must I leave to the world? Have you asked yourself that question lately? More importantly, have you answered the question? This book seeks to provoke you to answer the question by engaging in the work. I hope to give you ideas that will help you to accept and/or to extend the responsibility for giving back to others. This book will help you package your current existence into an energized, perpetual motion ENCORE LEADER!

HOW THIS BOOK IS STRUCTURED

One of the transitions that I have experienced as an Encore Leader is an appreciation for scholarly knowledge to support practical conclusions. Thus, I debated where the research that is the foundation for this book should be placed. To put it at the end felt as though it would minimize my passion for education. Putting it at the beginning would challenge the readers who care less about the scholarly research that evolved as the foundation for this book.

The compromise, as I modeled the work of Dr. Bell and Dr. Nkomo (2001), was to divide the book into sections with a research executive summary as Part I. This section includes the dissertation summary that provided the foundation for the development of the Encore Leadership process. (Foster, Cracking the Transition Code: A Paradigmatic Framework of Competencies that Construct the Reality of 50+ Black Executive Transitions, 2009)

If desired, the reader may quickly skip through the research and go immediately to the detailed discussion of the Encore Leadership process, Part II. Part III offers worksheet templates to get you started.

This book should be utilized as a resource guide. It attempts to acknowledge the work of masters who have studied and practiced various steps in the process of Encore Leadership. There are many theories and approaches to many of the steps, but choosing an approach or resource that works for an individual is the intent for engagement by readers of this book. Thus, providing readers with a flexible blueprint allows for choice by the Encore Leader to engage with other expert resources. There is not much that can be created on most topics that has not already been formulated. This book brings the key literature and practices to Encore Leaders. The extensive bibliography offers a summary of the literature that was explored in developing this book.

What is unique about the 12-step process is the specific focus to have Encore Leaders engage within a community to inspire their legacy work. Looking to move to legacy work that matters provides an opportunity to cycle to and through the leadership maturation life cycle to Encore Leadership!

PART I:

*CRACKING THE TRANSITION CODE
DISSERTATION EXECUTIVE SUMMARY*

THE RESEARCH FOUNDATION

OVERVIEW OF THE STUDY

Exploring the phenomenon of a group of individuals, who are living longer, with better health and greater resources offers an intriguing opportunity to accelerate contributions to organizations and society. 50+ is an age-based mindset that is attributed to these talented pioneers by AARP outgoing President, William D. Novelli (2006):

> We have a saying at AARP that age is just a number and life is what you make it. For Americans who are age 50 and over, the number is 50+ and the life you can make at that age has infinite possibilities. There's a thing about that plus sign: It means a whole lot more than "fifty-something" or "in her golden years" or "heading toward retirement." That plus sign means that more people are living longer and that people turning 50 today have more than half of their adult lives ahead of them. In fact, more and more people are actually turning 50 every day at a rate that's the highest in the history of the United States. A boomer turns 50 every 7.5 seconds. The plus sign behind that 50 also means that people thinking about retiring now have the opportunity to create a better quality of life, leave a legacy to our country, and ignite a revolution that will change the way we think about aging in America. The 50+ generation, just beginning to appear on the horizon, will ignite this revolution and change the United States in the process. (Novelli, 2006)

This research is conducted at a time when an unprecedented shift in the economic and socio-physiological stage of a major segment of the corporate population is occurring.

It is the best of times – the first African American President of the United States governs, and it is the worst of times – an economic meltdown with far reaching implications, driving the debt and future obligations that our children will inherit.

This study establishes a research framework to explore, discover, and contribute to the understanding of the transformation of organizations and society, using the lens of a participant group, i.e. Black 50+ executives. The past achievements, current endeavors, and future contributions of this network of individuals establishes a foundation for ongoing discovery and application of transition competencies that have been employed in their shift from first careers to second pursuits.

EXIGENCY FOR THE STUDY

A combination of factors piqued my interest in advancing this research. The four primary drivers for the study were: (a) capturing the implications of Black executives departing from corporations as an adult stage of life; (b) recording the history of this generation of corporate executives; (c) sharing with others the competencies that proved most helpful to Black executives when they transitioned from first careers to second pursuits; and, (d) exploring my personal experience with transitions.

Corporations often disregard the talent drain that professionals leave when their intellectual capital is retired. Individuals often fail to capture and restructure their lives in order to share their wisdom. Given that the participant group of Black executives represents a first generation demographic of talent departure from corporate entities, it is essential to establish research that captures this phase of their adult life and corporate history. The data examination has the potential to incent individuals to reapply their wisdom into second pursuits, as well as to add a talent pool for organizations to source opportunities where 50+ transitioned executives can uniquely contribute to projects and opportunities.

I am a 50+ Black corporate executive who transitioned from a successful first career to subsequent significant second pursuits. With self as actor, I was often contacted to share my story and to facilitate through executive coaching the transition of others. In addition, working with organization groups that were either affected by the membership transition of executives, or with organizations that were interested in transitioning executives as target markets for products and or services, it became of paramount interest to conduct this research. My curiosity in examining the unprecedented number of Black executives who have transitioned is to motivate greater and continued contributions of this generation of talent while providing insight for those yet to cross the bridge of transition.

Of equal importance, I have a personal desire to fill the void of diverse research participants who inform organization development literature by offering their authentic voices. These voices must be considered in order to strengthen the melting pot of organization development knowledge and achieve a more inclusive world environment, synchronized to the changes that are being encountered in the globally shrinking world of business. Including the voices of diversity is an important social, cultural responsibility as corporations and their leaders become global citizens, as opposed to simply becoming domestic recipients of the fruits of limited THINKing and visioning.

Reinventing people to lead innovative lives while committing to a greater level of personal responsibility is a desired outcome of this research. More than seventy study participants have made the transition from successful first careers to significant second pursuits in life. Their stories and insights define the transition competencies that accelerate the active engagement of the transition process, beyond traditional retirement and the necessity of fortuitous contributions. This research is needed both to imprint the historical legacy of the contributions of these individuals, and to inspire and motivate others to significant contributions in the back nine of life.

As I reviewed engagements with clients during the last nine years, I recognized the myriad of options that Black corporate executives were pursuing subsequent to leaving corporate careers. This research provides a significant introduction to the transition tipping points and competencies of this talented dataset, as well as generalizability potential for other 50+ participant sets. Individuals who navigate from first careers to second pursuits create a pool of talent that can quickly be deployed to engagement contributions that offer high levels of community consciousness in organization development and change.

Finally, this research is an unprecedented historical study of 50+ Black executives who have transitioned to second pursuits. The study offers a pathway for their future engagements while also asserting a pathway for those who follow. Building this bridge of understanding is a major contribution to individuals and to organizations.

The study attempts to build a bridge from the early careers of Blacks in corporate positions to the present day when the "Greatest Generation" (Brokaw, 1998) intersects with the "Bravest Generation of Blacks," featured on the cover of Fortune Magazine in August, 2005 (Daniels). Heralded as "Guts and Glory," the heartfelt stories of six Black pioneers who broke corporate America's color barrier in the 50s and 60s are shared. This brave generation inspired the "Boomer Generation," now on the cusp of their second significant pursuits following successful first careers.

One of the gentlemen profiled on the aforementioned Fortune cover had been a mentor and friend to me. It was a mentoring relationship that had but three points of intersection with each connection demonstrating a lifelong commitment to helping others, just as he had helped me during my first executive position as a Vice President at IBM, headquartered in New York City.

I met Darwin Davis, Senior Vice President at Equitable Life, at one of many IBM sponsored charitable events in New York City. After a discussion with Mr. Davis about my new position responsibility, he invited me to lunch in his office where we spent several hours discussing the New York environment and how to maximize my new opportunity. My final encounter with Darwin Davis was when I saw him at the Midway Airport in Chicago where he was arriving for a business meeting as I was departing. I stopped him and reintroduced myself. It was as if he remembered every word of our previous conversations; I was no stranger and I doubt that he ever knew a stranger; he did not put his SVP position before his being, or his identity. I committed to send him a copy of the book I had written, *Due North! Strengthen Your Leadership Assets*. I also remember I challenged him to write his story, as I believed it would be of great value to future Black executives.

I continue to cherish the handwritten letter that he wrote to me, postmarked, December 15, 2002. He had just started Darwin N. Davis Associates, Management Consultants. His words were poignant and continue to propel me forward…

> Coaching is the wave of the present and future and you and your book are right there. Timing is always everything, Jylla, so keep up the good work – again, proud of you girl, you're the best!!! Again thanks – Sincerely Darwin
>
> [The footer of the stationery: Darwin N. Davis, Senior Vice President, The Equitable –Retired.]

Mentoring and sharing stories became a reality for me with his passing on April 10, 2006. I realized, with a heightened sense of awareness, how small moments with giants could make a huge difference in life. If I can share his personal touch of caring with others, in concert with the caring of many other giants who have formed my being, it will ripple into works of significance during my second pursuits. I know that with his life as an example and the shared experiences of many other Black business heroes whom I have known, the bridge of practitioner scholar will be legacy work in which I can fulfill my God given talents.

Earl Graves, Sr., my "Father in Business" (Foster, 1998), also had tremendous respect for Darwin Davis. He proclaims him a keeper of the flame, who willingly stood in harm's way as an example for others to follow, and acknowledges his contributions of "working at Equitable, where he established a Black executive's support program; or in the community, where he contributed his time and money to everything from the Alvin Ailey dance troupe to the NAACP and the Urban League." (Sykes, 2009)

While Graves (1996, 1997) has always been the keeper of Black corporate history, he also personally demonstrated his commitment to mentoring and instilling the legacy of his dreams when he autographed a copy of his book to my daughter with these words:

To Anjylla

> You are part of a special family. Continue its history.
> Earl G. Graves, May 9, 1997

Anjylla is now a college graduate with degrees in International Business and Marketing and a master's degree in Communications. Fluent in Spanish, she continues her entrepreneurial interests. When she met Mr. Graves at a Kid-Preneur Conference, it was then that I recognized how legacies are created and I learned how significant work replicates and recreates itself for many generations. It is in regard to this concept that this research is conducted; so that many others will have influence in their second pursuits that will last throughout generations. This is a study of reinvention.

Numerous African Americans have transitioned, and continue to transition, from first careers to second pursuits. A common initial second pursuit that I have advocated is to document their stories. Examples of authors who have published their stories, or shared their nuggets of wisdom subsequent to my book, whom I have coached or consulted include: Chambers-Chima and Hunter (2005); Whaley (2004); Whaley (2004); Statum (2008); Arthur (2007); and several others. This attempt to mentor through sharing professional experiences and expertise is the give-back that has become synonymous with the transition journey. It is the area of future giving that I THINK will be significant to the multi-disciplinary contributions of talented Black professionals.

There is a fierce urgency of NOW related to this research. External forces that dictate the need for individuals to accept and transition to a firm sense of personal and professional responsibility are converging on organizations. We live in a time of unprecedented challenges and unparalleled change. It is truly the best of times and the worst of times. This is a tale of the United States, void of red state and blue state protection, but filled with the "audacity of hope" (Obama, 2006) and the "dreams of our fathers" (Obama, 1995/2004) and our mothers. It is a time when we must replicate the innovative stories of success.

Establishing a bridge that enables the journey of others to achieve success during transitions with the insight of those with experience and wisdom that have crossed the water to the other side of second pursuits is a significant contribution to organization development. I have crossed the bridge. More than seventy individuals who participated in this research have traveled different roads toward similar destinations. I wonder: Can my transition experience, coupled with the other 50+ Black executives, be framed within a conceptual construct that reveals the necessary competencies to successfully transition from first careers to second pursuits?

RESEARCH METHODOLOGY

After establishing the exigency for the study, extant literature was reviewed to understand what had been documented relative to competencies that executives deemed necessary for successful transitions. Literature existed in many streams that offered direction for further exploration. Yet, a gap for a unique niche of research surfaced; one that had not been explored, that is, the transition of 50+ Black executives.

To examine the question of transition competencies for 50+ Black executives, a research approach was engaged. The following schematic (See Figure 1) was used to guide the research process.

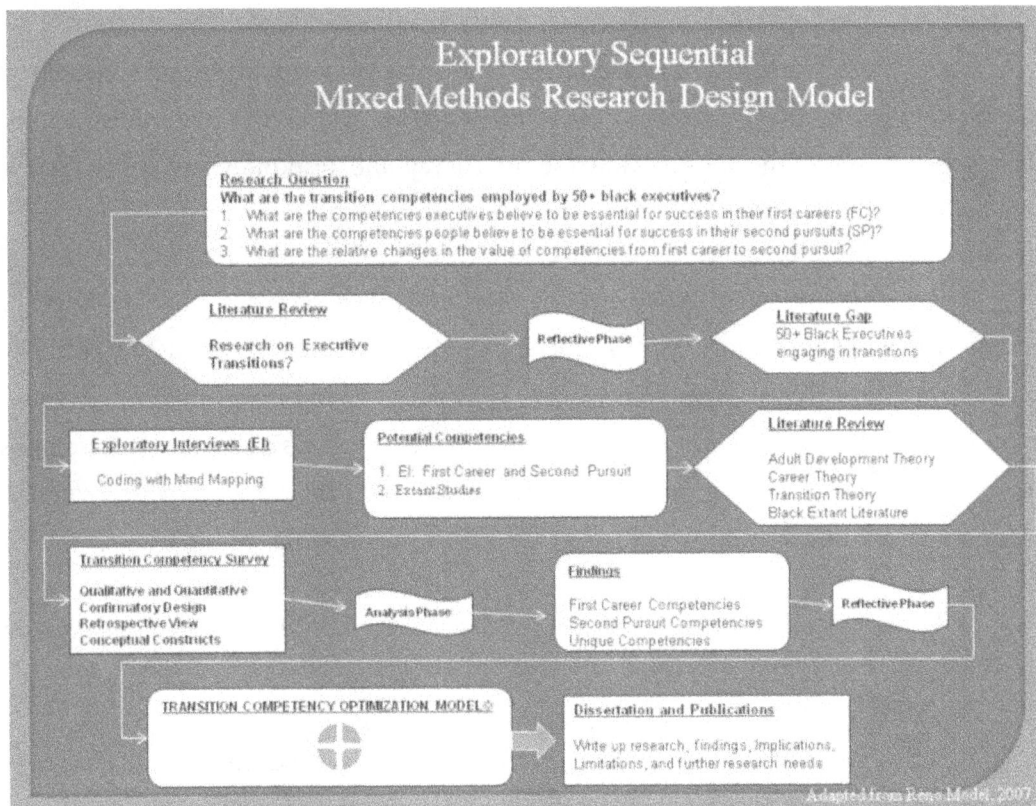

Figure 1. Exploratory Sequential Mixed Methods Research Design Model

Exploratory interviews were conducted with twenty professionals. An interview guide was developed that examined the nuances of 50+ transitions with an emphasis on what the professionals believed were essential competencies for first career and second pursuit transitions. (See Appendix A in the Dissertation, available at www. EncoreLeadership.com) An initial list of competencies was developed from the exploratory interviews and is documented in Appendix H of the Dissertation, available at www.EncoreLeadership.com.

A literature review was conducted to explore theories that were relevant to the transition competencies of 50+ Black executives. Adult development, career development, and transition theories were reviewed to determine the extant literature that attempted to explain this phenomenon. The literature review was very instrumental in formulating the conceptual categorical construct of the research approach. In addition, Black literature was a major component of the literature review given the participants that were selected for this study.

Utilizing the exploratory qualitative interview competencies and the theoretical literature review, a survey instrument was developed to explore the research questions. (See Appendix G in the Dissertation for the survey and responses available at www. EncoreLeadership.com).

The extensive transition survey that was developed provided both quantitative and qualitative data for analysis of the questions. Statistical analysis was used to identify the relative value executives placed on the competencies. Using a confirmatory design to assess competencies from previous studies that were reported as significant, the responses were analyzed using various statistical tests. In contrast, an exploratory study design identifies significant relationships (if any) from a list of proposed competencies.

Results provided analysis that helped assess what competencies were valued in second pursuits in addition to the first career.

Additionally, this study used a mixed retrospective and concurrent design in that participants were surveyed with two time elements for consideration. Questions were asked relative to the first career (FC) retrospectively and the second pursuit (SP) concurrently, which provided an opportunity to analyze the results based on two timeframes. In contrast, a prospective study would have surveyed participants at the start of their careers and then after the second pursuit. Because two time periods were rated by the participants, this study approximated a mixed retrospective and prospective design without waiting 20 years for careers to evolve. This framework offers the opportunity to both begin the development of research for various age groups while also tracking the progression of those who are engaged in their second pursuit. The integration of the findings from this approach is represented in the subsequent modeling that was engaged.

Based on the competencies determined for first career and second pursuit, a transition competency model was developed.

RESEARCH QUESTIONS

The following questions guided the research process and methodology that was used to examine the main objective of the study.

Primary question: What are the transition competencies employed by 50+ Black executives who transition from first careers to second pursuits?

Secondary questions:

1. What are competencies executives believe to be essential for success in their first careers?
2. What are the competencies executives believe to be essential for success in their second pursuit?
3. What are the relative changes in the value of competencies from first careers to second pursuit?

ANALYSIS AND FINDINGS

The research revealed twelve transition competencies that were essential to develop in first careers as anchors for second pursuits, and twelve transition competencies that are essential to master in the second pursuit. There was one competency that emerged as essential in both first careers and second pursuits, and four competencies that had significant declines from first careers to second pursuit.

The twelve transition competencies essential to develop in first careers as anchors for second pursuit are:

1. Building relationships
2. Influence
3. Trustworthiness
4. Character
5. Communication
6. Interpersonal relationships
7. Positive Attitude
8. Results orientation
9. "I Can" Credo
10. Self confidence
11. Adaptability
12. Follow through

The twelve transition competencies that are essential to master for successful second pursuit are:

1. Community Consciousness
2. Meaningfulness
3. Concern for form
4. Love of ideas
5. Gratitude
6. Spiritual
7. Life and Work Balance
8. Self Care
9. Inner Peace

10. Networking
11. Expression
12. Passion

The one competency that was significant in both first careers and second pursuit was performance. Competencies that had significant declines from first careers to second pursuit were career growth, adaptation to management/culture, beating competition, and competence.

The methodology used to examine the competencies provides a framework for further research with various participant sets and establishes a process to further the knowledge associated with this particular participant group, 50+ Black executives. It also offers a means to share transition knowledge with transitioning individuals who are interested in second pursuits.

A glossary of definitions for the competencies and the source of the competency, if applicable to a specific study, is included in Appendix I, available at www. EncoreLeadership.com.

BOUNDARIES AND LIMITATIONS OF THE STUDY

Given that this research had not been examined previously, it was necessary to establish boundaries for the initial study in order to conceptually construct the framework for transitions. In particular, specific guidelines were established that required participants to be 50+ years of age and Black corporate executives who were known to the researcher. Gender was not a specific delineator for consideration in this survey but leaves the door open for future research with focus on gender.

This study was framed with parameters that limited scope in order to align the conceptual constructs that emerged from the exploratory interviews, and the extant literature. The parameters were Black executives who are 50+ years in age, who have successfully transitioned from their first career to a second pursuit. First career was defined as a job or a series of jobs in a single corporation or multiple corporations that constitute the individuals' major work history prior to shifting to a second pursuit. The second pursuit is typically the work pursued after the first career. The second pursuit may include a primary shift from a corporate career to a leadership role in a non-profit, an entrepreneurial venture, volunteerism, or other areas of engagement. Given the preliminary and exploratory nature of the study, certain controls were not considered: type of second pursuit of the executives; whether the second pursuit choice had an effect on the study findings with respect to first career competencies; and, competencies required for transition from first career to second pursuit. These are questions for future extension of this research.

TRANSITION TIPPING POINTS

In 2005, Dr. Price Cobbs acknowledged his personal transformation as the March 25, 1965 march in Montgomery, Alabama. He noted that "for the first time in my adult life, really, I stepped away from my professional concerns and took to the streets." Engagement at this tipping point led him to recognize what he considered a sea change and to ask the question that was relevant to his THINKing:

> Are you participating personally in the issues of your time? I knew that from that moment on, my answer would be yes. There was to be no question about that. My participation was not to be on the periphery or extracurricular. I was not going to be just a psychiatrist, looking from afar at the issues of racism, age, and violence. I knew that I had to integrate all these issues into one thoughtful consciousness, and to act upon them. (Cobbs, 2005)

This seminal moment exemplifies the transformation of time, talent and treasure that identifies the characteristics of legacy work.

Malcomb Gladwell defined a tipping point as "the moment of critical mass, the threshold, the boiling point." (Gladwell, 2000) These triggers were identified through qualitative analysis using as a foundation, Mueller's Change Framework. (Mueller, 1978)

SECOND
CAREER
CHOICE

INTUITIVE MODE
OF PROBLEM SOLVING
AND DECISION MAKING

Refreezing

Consequences
Worries

Second-
Third
Thoughts

Choice
Winnow

Rationalization

Compromise

Gap
Recognition

ANALYTIC MODE
OF PROBLEM SOLVING
AND DECISION MAKING

Feasibility

Working
Criteria

Value
Setting

DESIRE
OR
NEED
FOR
CHANGE

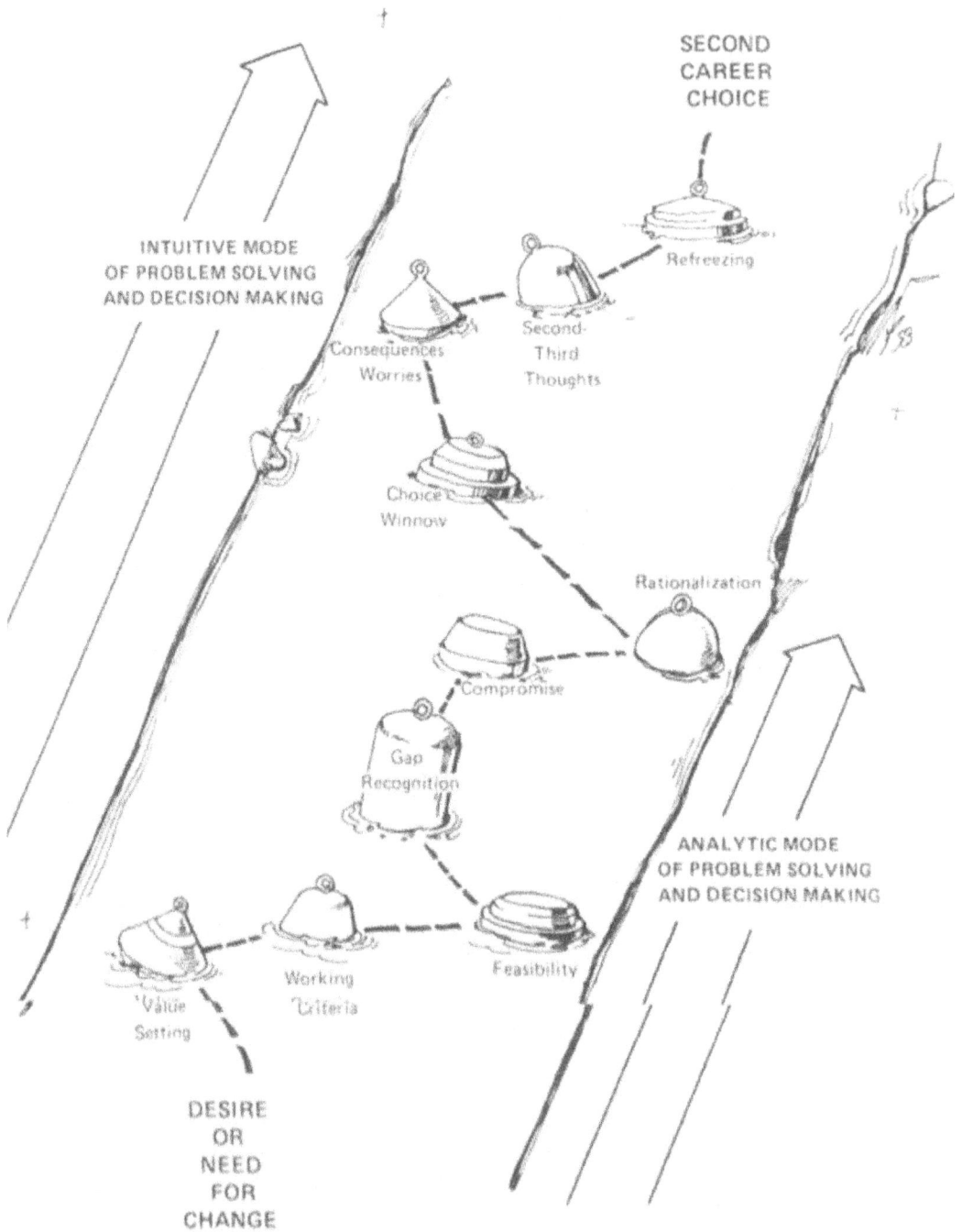

Figure 2. Mueller's Change Framework

The transition tipping points were queried with the transition survey qualitative and quantitative responses to various questions. Mueller's framework for career drivers was used as the initial framework for transition tipping points. The survey and mapping revealed three additional drivers for transition and eliminated one. The results in Table 1 of this book are presented in Table 30 of the Dissertation, available at www. EncoreLeadership.com.

Table 1. Transition Tipping Points Qualitative Summary

Driver	Survey Result
Alteration of environmental work setting	1. Was asked to relocate to Detroit—no way! 2. Considered the transformation of the company from a "branch office"-based organization that thrived on local relationships—to a "matrix organization"-based on skills and consulting deliverables. This new organization was more impersonal. Many that were going through the transition observed "this is not your father's IBM." 3. When we began another in a series of reorganizations, which resulted in my responsibilities being changed and reduced. 4. The MOT was when my last employer's CEO died prematurely (hired me) and the subsequent president did not have me in her plans (a former colleague) 5. After struggles with my then employer regarding my next career opportunity 6. I was about to launch a venture in August 2001. The attacks on 9/11 wiped out my business model.
Political Shift	1. Company shifted to public 2. Company merger 3. After the last downsizing, I realized the job was more stressful than fulfilling. I planned for a year. 4. Corporate reorganization 5. I pulled the plug and left my company during a merger because the individuals in the top senior positions that sponsored me left. Additionally, the company paid me a significant amount of money to do so.
Economic Shifts	1. Early retirement package 2. After my children were out of college and married, our financial needs as a family were drastically reduced and my retirement income was secure.

Table 1. Transition Tipping Points Qualitative Summary

Organization Climate	*14% Not enough challenge in responsibilities of first career*
	1. Creation of a value add, ethically-based company
	2. Sick and tired of incompetent management
	3. Toxic environment/culture
	4. Disagreement with account leadership
	5. After sitting in another fruitless, pointless meeting
	6. Treated unfairly following an illness
	7. Had enough of the politics, culture, and ineffectiveness of Corporate America
	8. There was too much inertia in the system and too many battles to fight to get anything done and I just didn't have the energy to take on the same old battles. I decided to focus on my exit plan knowing that I could easily complete the next 5 years. I changed my attitude and just focused on completing the work at hand, whatever that happened to be. This was a great attitude adjustment for me as I no longer worried about my future at IBM but focused on what it would be like after IBM. And it's been a great transition.
	9. The MOT was actually years in the making. Had been unhappy for a few years and began positioning to take an early retirement if available.
	10. Fully realized that I no longer had a passion for the work nor the company, rumors of additional RIF's offer additional options that were not of interest, called my mother said that I was done, she said good you have been miserable for a long time, just didn't "seem to enjoy what you're doing."
	11. Sitting in a meeting where I realized that everyone was either engaged or "pretending" to be engaged in a leadership development offsite.
	12. When I began to see that while I would retain some sort of autonomy in my work, the politics and stresses of working in a public firm (consulting) would not be to my liking.
	13. I knew my employer would be better served with me leaving.
	14. I had thought for years that 30 years with my company would be all I would do. Interestingly enough the last 7 years in sales learning were my most fulfilling years. I finally found my passion! Over time my desire to do it my way and not be involved in all the politics of a big company became my driving force
	15. Meeting with my supervisor and realizing that while my performance was good, the real opportunities were limited.

Table 1. Transition Tipping Points Qualitative Summary

Personal Matters	*37% Retirement eligible*
	35% Work Life Consideration
	9% Health Consideration

1. Retirement eligible, ill parents, personal desires
2. Along with very ill parents with whom I wanted to spend more time... when I made the decision, to the dismay of my upline management, it was liberating for me!
3. Money and not wanting to work to get new sponsors
4. Following an illness; no job (3)
5. One morning I asked myself if I was happy and if I enjoyed what I was doing... I could not answer yes anymore
6. Retirement (3)
7. Negotiated a bridge assignment
8. Realized could influence disadvantaged people through use of technology
9. MOT occurred during an encounter with my son's physician who felt that his medical condition was deteriorating (diabetes). This physician's pessimism about my son's future clinched my decision to stop working.
10. At that moment of truth, I decided to retire.
11. Feeling I had more to offer.
12. I decided it was time for me to retire
13. After 31 ½ years, I decided there was nothing else I wanted to do in that Corp career path.

Table 1. Transition Tipping Points Qualitative Summary

New Opportunity	*14% Personal interest in a new opportunity at another company*

1. New opportunity was not at another company
2. Interested in new "opportunity", not new company
3. When I was offered a job
4. Start a new business (4)
5. Accepted as vendor to the business I left; freedom of being on own; vendor to a client (5)
6. New opportunity derived from networking
7. New functional area of interest
8. Interest in Internet startup
9. Had a contract and money in the bank
10. After talking to a few people I highly regard and respect after they took their own leap to entrepreneurship
11. While on temporary assignment teaching, I realized that I loved teaching and the students needed me
12. The key moment of truth emerged when I realized that I was no longer passionate nor fully engaged with what I was doing. Other paths opened up that made moving on obvious and easy.
13. When I realized that I could transfer working for someone else to actually working for myself.
14. About 6 months prior to leaving, I knew what I wanted to do and knew that it needed to be my business. There was not one thing that led me to the decision, it was the natural evolution of a thought that had been building for years. When I realized my passion was in developing leaders, my objective was to prepare myself with the tools to be able to do this my way and my role offered me that opportunity.

Non-Voluntary	*33% Corporate resource action*

1. When I was terminated
2. After second experience of job elimination

Table 1. Transition Tipping Points Qualitative Summary

Career stabilized and security achieved	1. Wanting to have more of an impact and leave more of a legacy
	2. Compensation was most rewarding part of career and not the work, determined it was time to move on
	3. Just time
	4. Realized I did not have to go back to corporate
	5. Achieved goals of success shaped by corporate America with respect to responsibility, span of control, position within the firm, title, and compensation
	6. Although I have financial security, current retirement plans charge 10% penalty for funds withdrawn before 59 ½.
	7. Wondered after much corp success why I wasn't happier about it.
	8. There wasn't 1 moment. This has been an emerging transformation that holds several pivotal times/decisions. 1) the decision to leave the known and financial security of a "real job" for the financial surrendering into the unknown. 2) realization that I was being called to teach 3) Going back to school (MS, MOB, PhD), and 4) realizing that I loved the work of OD/change and loved learning/and advancing knowledge.
	9. I knew that I wanted to leave as soon as I was eligible to do so with a pension. I had plateaued in my career, the prospects for future advancement were uncertain and I didn't enjoy what I was doing.
	10. I had climbed the corporate leader for over 25 years. Goals and ambition always led me to the next position. I finally achieved all that I strived to accomplish. I decided to find a way to give back to society. This led me to a position in the public sector.

Table 1. Transition Tipping Points Qualitative Summary

Spiritual	
	1. Honoring a commitment I made to God Almighty
	2. Destiny confirmed with "trust me" awakening
	3. Holy Spirit shared He wanted me to leave corporate America by mid-fifties
	4. After seeing site of 9/11 in October 2001, "Called" to move to NY to see what was next
	5. God had given me the vision six months before for the name and focus for the business
	6. Wanted to create a company based on my own Christian-based values
	7. Realization that I was being called to teach
	8. I had a spiritual tug for starting a business off and on for 10 years.
	9. I made a promise with God after 15 years if He would let me remain in corporate America until I reach retirement, I would do His will and not take a penny for my service.
Dreams	
	1. "Trust me"
	2. Confusing dreams about being back at work

Table 1. Transition Tipping Points Qualitative Summary

Personal Realization	
	1. When I knew that I needed more purpose in the work that I was doing. I wanted to blend my reason for being and my talents with the work that I did.
	2. My current role working in the Middle East and Africa has opened me to all sorts of possibilities and even perhaps taking a more global approach to my second pursuit.
	3. Consider other options for the remainder of my life.
	4. So I decided it was time to do something to give back and something that would bring me more personal satisfaction.
	5. Always had an involvement with NFPs, usually on Board of Directors. MOT was several years before my transition when a neighbor made a similar transition and I saw the possibility.
	6. I felt nothing and acknowledged that I never would until I took the chance to pursue my entrepreneurial desires.
	7. The personal satisfaction from the first career diminished almost completely. The timing was right to make a change.
	8. I started my transition early in my career when I got my MBA. While getting the MBA I was able to work with individuals in the financial markets. I also felt that I needed multiple options. Options that gave me the ability to effectively deal with many of the race related career barriers African Americans had.
	9. During my first 3 week vacation with my wife and 2 young daughters (then 8 and 11 years old), I realized that the level of interpersonal interaction during the 2nd and 3rd weeks was keenly desirable and absolutely impossible as a senior investment banker. This was a traumatic realization. I DID NOT resign after returning from vacation but rather quietly shared my interest with a few search firms that were pursuing me for other investment banking roles that I would also welcome the right corporate role. My undergraduate degree was in Electrical Engineering from Stanford University and I had several years of successful experience with 2 large technology companies prior to business school.
	10. I determined that to reach my financial objectives, I would have to start my own consulting firm. I had no desire to pursue this option at that point in my life.
	11. Lack of African American professors in CIS

Abbreviation References: *MOT (moment of truth), RIF (reduction in force), NFP (not for profit), CIS (computer information systems).*

At a specific time with the confluence of several elements, one makes the decision, 74% by choice, 12% by force and 14% due to other factors, to transition to her or his second act in life.

The findings in the dissertation on "Cracking the Transition Code", offered the opportunity to present the data in the format of the Transition Competency Optimization Model©.

THE TRANSITION COMPETENCY OPTIMIZATION MODEL©

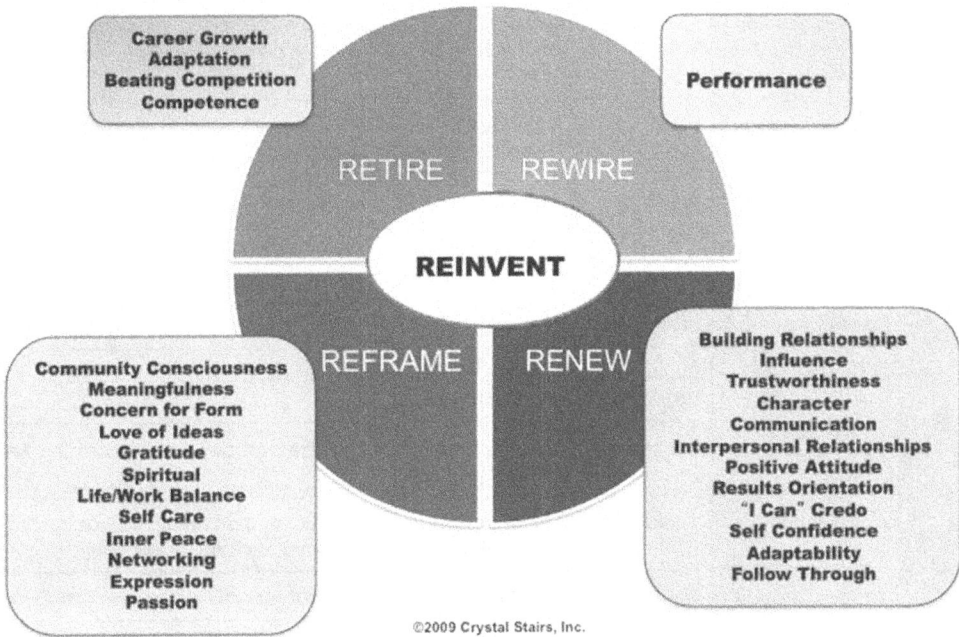

The model of transition that resulted from the detail study of transition is called the Transition Competency Optimization Model. This is the model that evolved which is a four-quadrant recognition of competencies.

The Transition Competency Optimization Model©

Career Growth
Adaptation
Beating Competition
Competence

Performance

RETIRE — REWIRE

REINVENT

REFRAME — RENEW

Community Consciousness
Meaningfulness
Concern for Form
Love of Ideas
Gratitude
Spiritual
Life/Work Balance
Self Care
Inner Peace
Networking
Expression
Passion

Building Relationships
Influence
Trustworthiness
Character
Communication
Interpersonal Relationships
Positive Attitude
Results Orientation
"I Can" Credo
Self Confidence
Adaptability
Follow Through

©2009 Crystal Stairs, Inc.

Figure 3. The Transition Competency Optimization Model©

The Transition Competency Optimization Model©

	COMPETENCY	CATEGORY	DEFINITION
RETIRE	Career Growth	Work Expectation	Concern with making progress toward professional goals
	Adaptation to management/ culture	Derailment	Concern with trouble in working with others and adjusting to different philosophies and strategies
	Beating Competition	Values	Values cluster of individualistic; emphasis on becoming number one, winning power, rising to the top
	Competence	Success Strategies	The difference between mediocrity and excellence; Must master one thing to perfection
RENEW (First Career)	Building Relationships	Skills	Interactions with others that result in continued connection and engagement
	Influence	Skills	Gains support and commitment from others to mobilize for action; use internal and external contacts to forge relationships; adds spark and vigor to work environment; gains alignment
	Trustworthiness	Skills	Establishes and maintains credibility with a variety of constituents by demonstrating consistency among principles, values, ethics and personal behavior; open and honest
	Character	Success Strategies	Open and honest in all business dealings with integrity as the basis for trust; earned
	Communication	Success	Effectively explain so that it taps one's sense of meaning; use of vivid images, voice tone, clarity of speech, clarity of THINKing
	Interpersonal Relationships	Derailment	Sensitive to others and appropriate level of ambition and behavior; engaged and network of people
	Positive Attitude	Success	Look at challenges as opportunities; Make best out of difficult situations; learn from and capitalizes on mistakes; appreciate making a difference; a sense of the possible
	Results Orientation	Success Strategies	Displays a commitment to and passion for achieving success; creates and tenaciously pursues objective and opportunities
	"I Can" Credo	Success Strategies	The positive mental attitude of acting as if you can vs. negative "I Can't"
	Self Confidence	Success Strategies	Knowing how to handle the worst by tapping into the deep reservoir of ability
	Adaptability	Success	Capable of becoming or being made suitable to a particular situation or use; being open to change; flexible
	Follow Through	Derailment	Keeps promises, says what means and delivers; trusted

Figure 4. Retire and Renew Competency Definitions

The Transition Competency Optimization Model©

	COMPETENCY	CATEGORY	DEFINITION
REFRAME (Second Pursuit)	Community Consciousness	Values	Social values cluster; performing volunteer work, sacrifice own needs for others; great lengths to eliminate global conflict and hate
	Meaningfulness	Success	Having function or purpose, being highly focused, maintaining principles
	Concern for form	Values	Exemplified by desire for harmonious relationships, beautiful surroundings, an interest in personal growth and creative expression; anticipates life's experiences; Aesthetic values cluster
	Love of ideas	Values	Theoretical values cluster; thirst for information on wide range of subjects for sake of information itself; rational debater, sharp critical thinking skills
	Gratitude	Success	Thankfulness; often results in giving back and helping others
	Spiritual	Life Attributes/ Success Strategies	"The inner urge of the Divine presence in mankind urging you and me to release our talents and express more and more of God's force." - Kimbro
	Life and Work Balance	Derailment	Balances work priorities with personal life so that neither is neglected
	Self Care	Life Attributes	Prioritizing personal well being
	Inner Peace	Success	Ability to focus and achieve when calm; less stressed, frenetic, more self aware and more in harmony
	Networking	Skills	Building, maintaining and nurturing relationships with others
	Expression	Work Expectation	Sharing your opinions and feelings openly
	Passion	Success Strategy	Find your place and overfill it; Set "yourself on fire so the world will come to see you burn." - King
REWIRE	Performance	Derailment (-) PIE (+)	Handles situations appropriately with demonstrated consistent skill (Derailment) Achievement level of the objectives as set forth for the job or responsibility using both known and unknown measurement criteria

Figure 5. Reframe and Rewire Competency Definitions

DEFINITIONS OF THE TRANSITION COMPETENCY MODEL

The definition of each of the attributes in the model is provided in Figure 4 and Figure 5.

SOURCES OF THE FACTORS WITHIN THE CATEGORIES

To develop the model, several sources were utilized with extant literature serving as a foundation to categorize the research findings. The sources are identified in Figure 6.

MAPPING FACTORS WITHIN CATEGORIES TO TRANSITION COMPETENCIES

Integrating the factors with the categories defined will ensure that the necessary areas for focus in transition are included as an individual reinvents herself. This model is competency driven and thus, it is critical to have a sense for the connection to how one masters transition skills that may be different from previous mastered skills. Figure 7 provides the mapping framework.

Reinvention invites the opportunity to continue to expand knowledge and skills that position one for greater success in their area of passion.

Sources of the Factors within the Categories

Category	RENEW 1st Career	REWIRE 1st to 2nd	RETIRE 1st and 2nd	REFRAME 2nd Career
Skills	Building Relationships Influence Trustworthiness Results Orientation			Networking
Derailment Factors	Interpersonal Relationships Follow Through	Performance (-)	Adaptation to Management/Culture	Life and Work Balance
Success	Communication Positive Attitude Adaptability		Competence	Meaningfulness Gratitude Inner Peace
Success Strategies	Character "I Can" Credo Self Confidence			Spiritual Passion
Values			Beating Competition	Community Consciousness Concern for Form Love of Ideas
Life Attributes				Spiritual Self Care
Work Expectations			Career Growth	Expression
PIE		Performance (+)		

Documents referenced (See dissertation for complete citations)

Skills: Fortune 500 Firm (I)
Derailment Factors: Fortune 500 (II)
Success: Goodly, Neff/Citrin
Success Strategies: Kimbro
Values: Judy Suiter's Book based on Values Profile of Target Training International
Life Attributes: Life Options Assessment
Work Expectations: Inscape Publishing Assessment
PIE: Harvey Coleman's Book, Performance, Image, Exposure

Figure 6. Sources of the Factors within the Categories

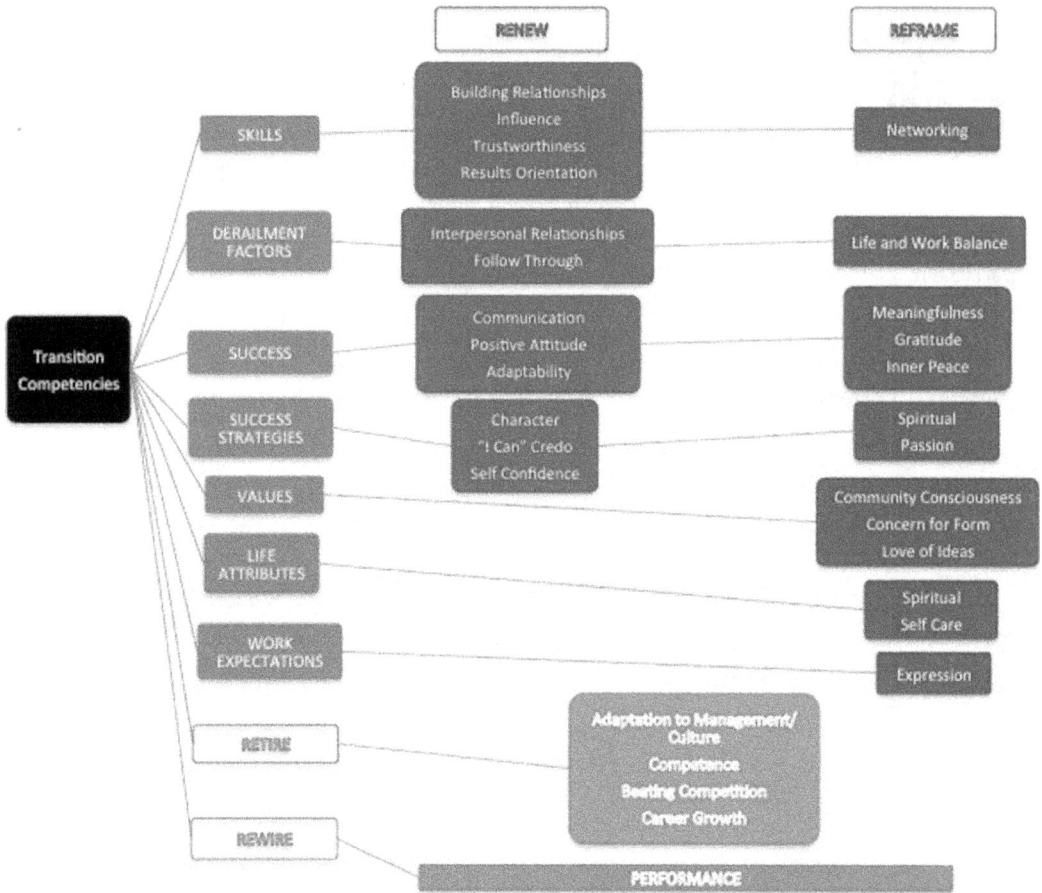

Figure 7. Mapping Factors within categories to Transition Competencies

DISCUSSION OF THE TRANSITION COMPETENCIES

Twelve competencies were identified in the research that are critical to successfully transition into an Encore Leadership life. Reframing and gaining clarity relative to these areas of focus requires creating a vision for the future that honors your past while creating environments for future visioning. THINKing about questions related to each of these competencies is the launch pad for shifting the focus on reinventing life. Consider the questions and THINK about your reflections and responses.

The competencies identified as necessary to reframe for second pursuits are:

1. Community Consciousness
2. Meaningfulness
3. Concern for Form
4. Love of Ideas
5. Gratitude
6. Spiritual
7. Life and Work Balance
8. Self Care
9. Inner Peace
10. Networking
11. Expression
12. Passion

1. COMMUNITY CONSCIOUSNESS

Social values cluster; performing volunteer work, sacrifice own needs for others; great lengths to eliminate global conflict and hate.

- What do you care about related to the community in which you consider yourself a citizen?
- What information do you need to gain knowledge about community issues that you could assist in addressing?
- How do you want to impact your community?
- What are three steps that you could take in the next 90 days to impact your community?
- Who should you discuss your interest with?
- When will you meet with your community partner?

2. MEANINGFULNESS

Having function or purpose, being highly focused, maintaining principles.

- Who are you?
- When you wake up in the morning, what is your purpose?
- How do you introduce yourself to others?
- What matters to you in life?
- What do you want individuals to remember about meeting you?
- How can you strengthen your redefined introduction?
- What principles do you uphold?

3. CONCERN FOR FORM

Exemplified by desire for harmonious relationships, beautiful surroundings, an interest in personal growth and creative expression; anticipates life's experiences; Aesthetic values cluster.

- Which relationships matter in your life?
- Where do you go to enjoy solitude and quiet time?
- How do you invoke your personal space?
- What is your approach to lifelong learning?
- What are you currently learning?
- How are you personally growing?
- What is your outlet for creative energy?
- What life experience are you anticipating?

4. LOVE OF IDEAS

Theoretical values cluster; thirst for information on wide range of subjects for sake of information itself; rational debater, sharp critical thinking skills.

- How do you keep your tool-kit sharpened?
- What are you adding to your knowledge base?
- What subject matter is of interest to you?

- How do you keep up to date with current events and knowledge?
- Who is your debate partner? Your THINKing partner? Your Board?

5. GRATITUDE

Thankfulness; often results in giving back and helping others.

- What are you thankful for?
- Who have you expressed gratitude to most recently? How?
- Who is overdue for your expression of gratitude? What will you do? When?
- What random act of kindness have you extended today?

6. SPIRITUAL

"The inner urge of the Divine presence in mankind urging you and me to release our talents and express more and more of God's force. " - Kimbro

"The key to spiritual enlightenment is overcoming our attachments." - Leider and Shapiro

- How do you engage with your spiritual being?
- How do you give fuel to your spirituality?
- How do you share your spiritual being with others?
- When does your talent intersect with your spirituality?
- How does your spiritual being differ from your religious being?

7. LIFE AND WORK BALANCE

Balances work priorities with personal life so that neither is neglected.

- What is your life work equation?
- What is your work life equation?
- How do you manage the equation?
- What are you neglecting in life? In Work?
- What is out of kilter with your work? Your life?

- How do you consciously shift the equation?
- What will you do today to invoke a shift?

8. SELF CARE

Prioritizing personal well-being.

- What is most important to your well-being?
- How are you intentionally focused on self-care?
- What are you doing to maintain the priorities of your well-being?
- Who can help you progress to greater well-being?

9. INNER PEACE

Ability to focus and achieve when calm; less stressed, frenetic, more self aware and more in harmony.

- When you go to sleep at night, do you have any regrets?
- Are there any apologies that you need to extend?
- What gives you peace?
- What can you do to gain greater inner peace?
- How do you calm your THINKing? Your physical being?
- How do you manage stress?
- What stress can you eliminate from your life? What must you do?
- How can you gain greater harmony in life?

10. NETWORKING

Building, maintaining and nurturing relationships with others.

- What are your relationship circles?
- How do you consciously stay connected?
- What is your plan to systematically nurture your network?
- What event do you plan to attend that will strengthen your network?

- Who do you need to re-establish a trusted relationship with?
- Which organization can you make a greater contribution to?

11. EXPRESSION

Sharing your opinions and feelings openly

- What have you not said that needs to be said?
- What have you said that you should have kept to yourself?
- How do you determine when your voice is a critical factor to express?
- When did you wish you had spoken up?
- Who needs to hear your voice?

12. PASSION

Find your place and overfill it; Set "yourself on fire so the world will come to see you burn."
- Dr. Martin Luther King, Jr.

- What do you care about?
- What wakes you up in the morning?
- What would you do 24x7 without pay?
- How do you engage with your passion?
- How do you define your passion?
- How does your passion fuel your purpose?

Revisit your responses to these questions on a frequent basis to give your reinvention the focus and attention that it will require. Share your thoughts with others. Add dimensional THINKing to your approach by exploring literature, listening to lectures, engaging in organizations, attending events outside your comfort zone, and shifting your environmental presence.

The Encore Leadership Model includes a myriad of competencies that must be integrated for a successful shift to the next stage of life. Rewire your performance. How will you measure your success? What matters?

Renew your "first career" skill set identified in the following list and apply them to your Encore Leadership life.

1. Building Relationships
2. Influence
3. Trustworthiness
4. Character
5. Communication
6. Interpersonal Relationships
7. Positive Attitude
8. Results Orientation
9. "I Can" Credo
10. Self Confidence
11. Adaptability
12. Follow Through

Retire the thoughts and competencies of career growth, adaptation to management/culture, beating competition and competence. Maintain your high regard for performance. In your Encore Leadership life, you have a blank sheet of paper to create the life that you envision. Leave the baggage of self-inflicted guilt and barriers and move forward to the world you desire.

PART II:

THE ENCORE LEADERSHIP PROCESS©

OVERVIEW

The process of Encore Leadership explores a 4-phase approach driven by a tipping point that ignites 12 steps of transformation for Encore Leaders.

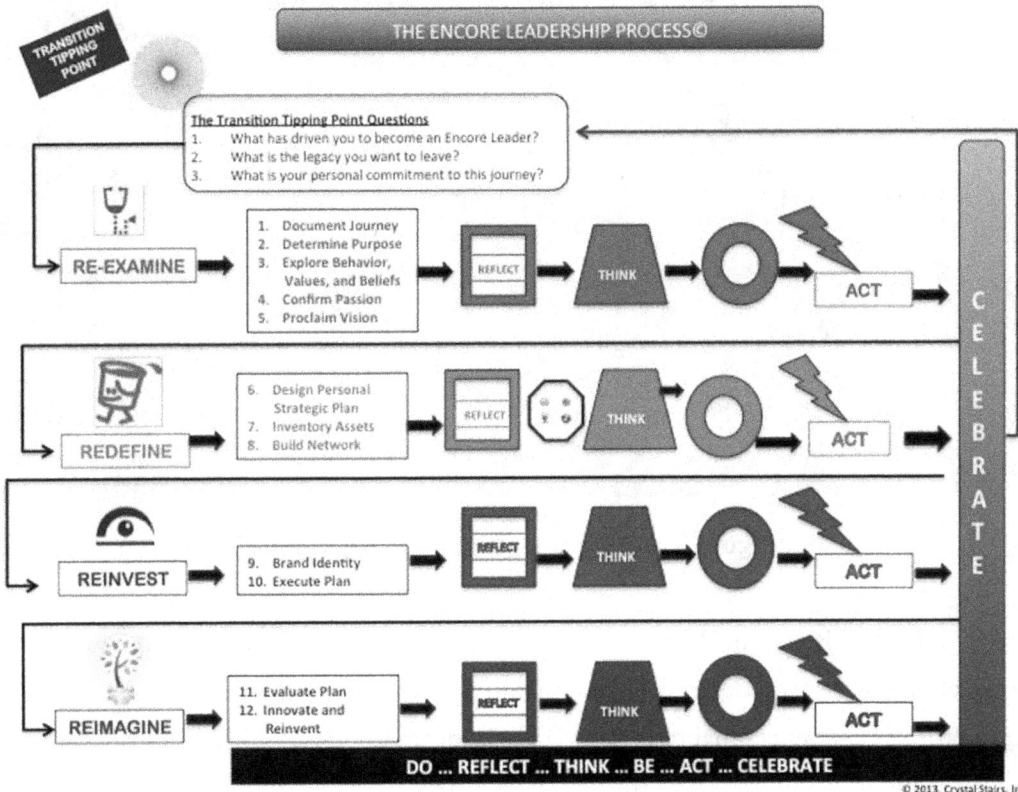

Figure 8. The Encore Leadership Process©

THE LEADERSHIP MATURATION LIFE CYCLE©

Recognizing Encore Leader as a specific stage of leadership requires concerted energy to define and to bring it to life. Whether the means is through the structured engine of AARP and/or grassroots building with Crystal Stairs, Inc., this is a pivotal concept in extending the stages of leadership development. Thus, the critical introduction of the leadership maturation life cycle is a fundamental branding of this next stage of adult engagement that is currently being designed and executed by Encore Leaders and progressive adults.

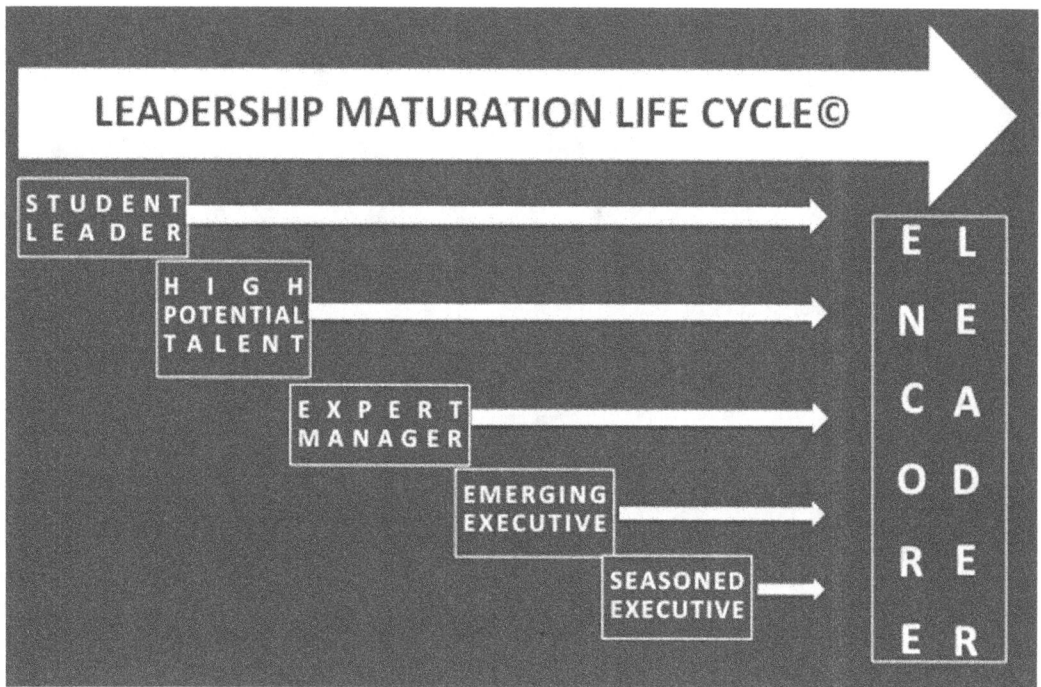

LEADERSHIP MATURATION LIFE CYCLE©

STUDENT LEADER

HIGH POTENTIAL TALENT

EXPERT MANAGER

EMERGING EXECUTIVE

SEASONED EXECUTIVE

ENCORE LEADER

Figure 9. Leadership Maturation Life Cycle©

While this graphic depicts my experience, the implications are more far reaching. Imagine shifting the model to your personal life cycle. For example, as a mother, you may have various experiences that have led to becoming an Encore Leader. They may include: PTA President or Sorority/Fraternity President; putting your career track on hold to be a stay-at-home parent and the chief social family architect; becoming an expert home manager; being the supportive family member for those climbing the corporate ladder; mastering the role of hostess extraordinaire by entertaining global clients or Bishops visiting your local church; to pursuing a re-invented life, utilizing your latent talent and shifting the time and treasures that you have acquired. What is your story of leadership that has positioned you to explore the concept of Encore Leadership?

Ginny Clarke meticulously defined the encore level of career mapping with the following definition that inspired my notion of an Encore Leadership process and this specific stage of leadership:

> Encore Level: Typically a person who is approaching retirement age (age 55 or older), regardless of station or level. He or she might be seeking to stay active and competitive in the workforce, or may be looking to move out of a traditional role and into another area of interest or passion, either compensated or as a volunteer. (Clarke & Garrett, 2011)

Throughout her book, Clarke provides references to the encore level of career mapping, which can be instructive as we develop our personal strategic vision when mapped to our career goals and objectives.

Leider and Shapiro offer that "all jobs have 'lives': cycles of learning, mastery, plateauing, and declining." (2012, p. 88) Recognizing these stages within the process of maturing as a leader can often serve as a clue that a transition is approaching.

This is the tipping point of transition. When you recognize that you want to shift to legacy work that matters, the process of re-inventing your life becomes the renewed energy for your life.

How do you know when you're in transition? Burton and Wedemeyer (1991, p. 29) offer that transition is:

- A time to grow in self-acceptance – to take more satisfaction from your skills and attributes and become less preoccupied with your short suits;

- A time to build the next chapter of your professional life on a firm foundation – on your core values, your immediate priorities, and your cherished skills;

- A time to regain balance in your life.

Buford offers a series of questions that assist in provoking THINKing regarding the "halftime of life." (1994, pp. 70-71) The questions that you should consider are:

1. What do I want to be remembered for?
2. What about money? How much is enough? If I have more than enough, what purpose do I serve with the excess?
3. How am I feeling about my career now? Is this what I want to be doing with my life ten years from now?
4. Am I living a balanced life? What are the important elements in my life that deserve more time?
5. What is the primary loyalty in my life?
6. Where do I look for inspiration, mentors, and working models for my second half?
7. Peter Drucker says that two important needs are self-realization and community. On a scale of 1-10 (10 being the highest), how am I doing in these areas?
8. Draw a line that describes the ups and downs of your life. Or draw three lines, one for personal life, one for family life, and one for work life. Where do they intersect? Where do they diverge?
9. Which of the following transition options seems to fit my temperament and gifts best? (Evaluate each option on a scale of 1-10.)
   a. Keep on doing what I already do well, but change the environment.
   b. Change the work, but stay in the same environment.
   c. Turn an avocation into a new career.
   d. Double-track (or event triple-track) in parallel careers (not hobbies).
   e. Keep on doing what I'm doing, even past retirement age.
10. What do I want for my children?

Guidelines for a successful journey during halftime are offered by Buford. (2000, p. 86) The guidelines suggest:

1. Make peace with your first half issues.
2. Take time for the things that are really important.
3. Be deliberate.
4. Share the journey.
5. Be honest.
6. Be patient.
7. Have faith.

THE TRANSITION TIPPING POINT

When one hits the inevitable "Transition Tipping Point," shifts will occur by design or by happenstance. Controlling destiny is somewhat of an oxymoron that can be maneuvered with a plan. That is the purpose of providing this insight on re-inventing life so that sharing experiences, techniques, and approaches can ultimately increase the contributions of Encore Leaders to society.

De Bono (2009) posits that *"we live over time. New information comes in over time. We add this new information to what we already have. There may come a point where we have to go back and restructure what we had before. This is creativity"*. Transition, when viewed through the lens of creativity, opens up a view of the world that may never have been anticipated. It cleans the slate to explore and design a re-created way of being.

Exercising your creative abilities is a learned process. In *Creativity Workout*, De Bono (2008) provides several exercises that can be engaged to facilitate creativity. The exercises relate to the following categories:

- Values
- Problem Solving
- Needs
- Enjoy
- Simplify

This can be a fun yet instructive approach to THINKing out loud about your Encore Leadership life while seeking light bulbs that may be switched on during the process.

Combined with the ability to adapt De Bono's "lateral thinking" concepts to transitions, (1985) and (1970), it is important to weave in various modalities of thoughts. In conversation pods, one can explore the aspects of facts and figures, emotions and feelings, caution, constructive criticism, focus and creative THINKing. Deep dives into the various THINKing patterns could offer the freedom to unearth the Encore Leadership life at the transition tipping point.

TRANSITION TIPPING POINT VOCABULARY

The tipping point inspires a new vocabulary. Defining the new words that will guide your journey is your first opportunity to reposition your life. Explore and document your definitions and compare/contrast to the definitions that are provided as guideposts in this book in Appendix A.

TERM	YOUR ENCORE LEADERSHIP DEFINITION
Encore Leader	
Legacy Voice	
Change	
Transition	
Transformation	
Success	
Significance/Significant	
Vision	
Purpose	
Passion	
Behavior	
Values	
Beliefs	
Meaningfulness	
Mattering	

These are just a few words and concepts that will become the future language for Encore Leaders. The more open your road ahead, the more driven you will be. The cleaner the white paper to etch your map is, the more creative your journey will be. The more receptive you are to exploring your mindset, the more creative and innovative your journey will be.

ENCORE LEADERSHIP MINDSET

There are seven mindsets that I THINK are key for Encore Leaders to adopt. They are:

1. Having "An Attitude of Gratitude"
2. Striving for Success and Significance
3. Sharing Wisdom
4. Mattering
5. Appreciating Solitude
6. Knowing your "Good Life"
7. Valuing the Freedom to Choose

1. HAVING "AN ATTITUDE OF GRATITUDE"

Keith Harrell first introduced me to the power of attitude through his profound presentation and his written word. Gone too soon, Keith was a trainer extraordinaire. His legacy lives on with his books, *Attitude is Everything* (2000), an *Attitude of Gratitude* (2003) and *Attitude is Everything for Success* (2004). Keith's passion for his work was exemplified in every step of his life journey, which was sprinkled indelibly with his positive mental attitude.

Keith was a former top-training instructor at IBM. He left to pursue his passion, which was speaking on the subject that he mastered: ATTITUDE. He offered 10 steps for turning attitude into action, which intersect at several points with the 12 steps to Encore Leadership:

1. Understand the Power of Attitude
2. Take Control of Your Life

3.   Practice Self-Awareness
4.   Re-Frame Your Bad Attitude
5.   Find Your Purpose and Passion
6.   Be Pre-Active
7.   Discover How to Motivate Yourself
8.   Build Supportive Relationships
9.   See Change as an Opportunity
10. Leave a Lasting Legacy

Encore Leaders must focus on the adoption of an attitude that is obvious to others. The work to develop an attitude of gratitude at this stage of life requires that one focus on a positive approach to living and being. John Maxwell offers very instructive means to engage in this work as the first chapter in his book, *Make Today Count.* (2004) Consciously deciding that you will approach your day with a positive attitude, including positive THINKing in your conversations and attempting to find ways to demonstrate your "Positive Mental Attitude (PMA)" as taught to me by Greg Wylie, former IBM Marketing Executive, provides fuel that keeps the day energized and exciting. Maxwell shared a very relevant prayer that he discovered as it relates to Encore Leaders:

Dear Lord,

So far today, I am doing all right. I have not gossiped, lost my temper, been greedy, grumpy, nasty, selfish, or self-indulgent. I have not whined, cursed, or eaten any chocolate.

However, I am going to get out of bed in a few minutes, and I will need a lot more help after that. Amen. (Maxwell, 2004)

Patricia Russell-McCloud asserts that "attitude determines your altitude, how high you will fly in this life." (1999) Once a person changes her attitude, the door of transformation opens. This undergirding of attitude that calls for Encore Leaders to exhibit an attitude of gratitude is offered with the hope that they will propel themselves into a life that is not hindered by boundaries that are self-inflicted attitudinal adjustments that are waiting to happen.

Maurice Arthur shared the realization of the viewing of the "purple mountains majesty" in his recount of his family ski trip. He also utilized the example of skiing down a difficult slope with his son to seize the opportunity for attitude to change one's view. The experience left him with the lesson that he shared in his book that "controlling your attitude can enhance your confidence." (Arthur, 2007) Defining your Encore Leadership attitude will give you the confidence to explore the possibilities of the next phase of life.

Gratitude is defined as "Thankfulness; often results in giving back and helping others" in the reframing of the transition competencies. Former President Bill Clinton discusses "Giving" in his book (2007) to share how each of us can change the world. He introduces his book with the statement:

> When I left the White House, I knew I wanted to spend the rest of my life giving my time, money, and skills to worthwhile endeavors where I could make a difference. I didn't know exactly what I would do, but I wanted to help save lives, solve important problems, and give more young people the chance to live their dreams. (Clinton, 2007)

In an interview with Vicki Hitzges, Motivational Strategist, she states that "people who are ungrateful rarely feel happy in life while those who find reasons to give thanks usually feel joy." (2013) She reminds us of Oprah's declaration to keep a "Gratitude Journal". Another step to truly develop an attitude of gratitude.

"It is more blessed to give than to receive" is a mantra for life that has been followed by many of the Christian faith for centuries. This is an attitude of gratitude that invites a spirit of sharing and caring that validates the approaches offered by many individuals who seek to share their positive mental attitude on a daily basis as they walk through each phase of the leadership maturation life cycle with Encore Leadership as a destination.

2. STRIVING FOR SUCCESS AND SIGNIFICANCE

Nightingale defines success as *"the progressive realization of a worthy ideal."* (1956) Embellished in his words is the notion of time and goals. As one redefines success for the Encore Leadership life it is key to keep in mind that it will take time, but one should be focused on an end game.

Qubein (1997, p. 1) describes success as "not a matter of luck, an accident of birth, or a reward for virtue. It is a matter of decision, commitment, planning, preparation, execution and recommitment. Success doesn't always come to you; you must go to it."

With these definitions as the foundation for success, it grounds the THINKing of the shift from success to significance. The recommitment phase of success often launches one into work that truly matters. Qubein offers that when a person reaches a "long-sought plateau, they immediately create their next vision." (1997, p. 3) This cycle of success spins into significance. When the questions shift, when the focus changes, when clarity is gained… life is transformed. It shifts to work that really matters. Legacy work.

No longer are the questions about fame and fortune. Rather, the questions before more about serving others and what will be written in our final chapter of life. Things become less important than the time we spend with our family and friends. Our spirituality encompasses our mind, body and souls. Our heart strings are tugged by those who truly make a difference in our lives.

Success takes a back seat to significance.

Jot down the three key shifts that you believe represent your shift from success to significance, whether obtained or aspirational.

1.

2.

3.

Bob Buford has mastered "Halftime." He has published numerous books on the subject that are extremely instructive. In his book, *Halftime: Changing Your Game Plan from Success to Significance* (1994), he offers the following insight as one embarks on the journey:

1. Make peace with the first half without regrets by overcoming them through grace;
2. Take time on the things that are really important;
3. Be deliberate in structuring your next half;
4. Share the journey with someone who is committed to travel with you;
5. Be honest, authentic and realistic with your expectations;
6. Be patient with your journey;
7. Have faith in what you hear when you listen and trust.

Leider and Shapiro offer provocative dialogue on success.

Satisfaction always leads to dissatisfaction; that's human nature. It's very difficult to sustain passion for something you've been involved in for many years – whether that's a job, a relationship, or a community. Success always becomes routine and mechanical; that's how it becomes success in the first place. So you have to reinvent yourself. You have to dream of something new to revitalize the old original feelings of aliveness. (Leider and Shapiro, 2012, p. 151)

3. SHARING WISDOM

Sharing wisdom is a means of giving. Wisdom is *"being able to access what's really important in the moment."* (Leider & Shapiro, 2004, p. 86) Aspiring to share wisdom is a cornerstone of maturing. Through many centuries, we have appreciated the wisdom of our elders.

I distinctly remember a conversation with Dr. E. Fran Johnson when I was working on my dissertation, and she shared with me thoughts on wisdom. It was poetic, yet a conversation. The words were provocative, yet simple. The impact was forever, even though the phone call was only a few minutes in time. When words collide to take you to a higher purpose in life, you have learned at the feet of a wise elder. Can you recall a moment in time when you knew you were touched by the wisdom of an elder in a profound way?

As you craft the next phase of life after you have reached your tipping point, one method to assess your time and energy is to reflect on the way you choose to lead your life. I have consciously and intentionally chosen to spend my time by investing in my Faith, my Family by loving and living in service to others. How do you choose to live your life?

A lecture by Professor Randy Pausch at Carnegie Mellon University inspired Zaslow's writing of the book, *The Last Lecture* (2008). As Pausch pondered how to leave a legacy for his children that taught them his values and beliefs, he decided to craft his "last lecture." He answered the question, what wisdom would we impart to the world if we knew it was our last chance? Professors have routinely been asked to lecture on the topic of the question, but for Pausch, this last lecture was, in fact, his last.

Pausch exercised while working with Zaslow, and their conversations were turned into fifty-three lectures. He thought it important to share thoughts on:

- Really achieving your childhood dreams
- Overcoming obstacles
- Enabling the dreams of others
- Seizing every moment
- Living

Discerning your contributions to others can assist in determining your confidence in your wisdom giving and wisdom seeking. What wisdom would you impart in your last lecture?

4. MATTERING

The concept of mattering evolves as one continues to mature through the leadership life cycle. The desire to truly make a difference becomes center stage in life. Questions surface relative to if the work that one does on a daily basis really matters. We begin wondering if and how the work will impact the life of someone else. At some point, mattering becomes a major desire for Encore Leaders. They are challenged to capture the moments of intersecting beliefs with actions. Encore Leaders must confront purpose and live their beliefs.

> Purpose is not a matter of theology. Our beliefs about the hereafter are not what ultimately matter. What matters is whether we live out our beliefs. Or as Stephen Levine puts it in Who Dies?: "Death is not the enemy. The enemy is ignorance and lovelessness."
>
> The reason why the issue of purpose is so important to a vital second half of life is that it raises issues that, ultimately, are inevitable. None of us is going to get out of this life without facing the question "Why am I here?" None of us is going to be able to avoid confronting the question of our life's meaning. We don't really get away with not wondering what our legacy will be after we're gone.
>
> By thinking intentionally about our life's purpose – by thoughtfully reflecting on our life's meaning – we give ourselves the time and space to think about things that sooner or later we're going to have to think about, whether we want to or not. And if we do this well and do it with intention, we can define our life's purpose and reclaim it so that we are able to integrate it successfully in all that we do throughout the second half of our lives. New elders do this and do so in ways that make their lives more vital for themselves and for family friends, and, in many cases, clients and customers as well. (Leider & Shapiro, 2004, pp. 112-113)

I found the dialogue by Frederic in *Claiming Your Place at the Fire* to be very thought provoking. He shared:

> Recently while looking for something else, Frederic started recycling his vast library of books to places he felt would like them. 'Clearing those shelves

heartens me," he says. "In going through my books, I wanted to unearth some answers to this question: 'What do we need to become an elder? Living in that question, I'm releasing all the ideas I no longer need which is most of them. In all ways, I want to enter this elder phase of life carrying as little as possible – unpacking as you say: That way my mind, hands, and heart will be free to be." (Leider & Shapiro, 2004, p. 105)

Leider and Shapiro continue:

Meaningful work, at any stage of life, is work through which we express our calling on projects about which we are passionate. (Leider & Shapiro, 2004, p. 87)

Rev. T. D. Jakes offers a perspective of mattering as he reflected on the life of his mother and the power of the legacy that she left. (Jakes, 2002, p. 228)

His testimony provides a moment of reflection. Use this space to jot down thoughts of how the work that you do matters.

_____

_____

_____

_____

What is the legacy that will result from your work?

_____

_____

_____

_____

5. APPRECIATING SOLITUDE

"Where are your places of quiet where the universe can be contemplated with awe?" (Leider & Shapiro, 2012, p. 50) A listening point is described as "a place to unpack and be fully ourselves." Larry Christie captures his listening point as "his spiritual refuge, where the good life prevails." Leider describes his listening point as the place where he can "tap into the slower rhythm. I can move into the feel of the river, which carries me along at its own steady pace. I'm able to see the gentle flow of the water, hear the wind through the trees, and at the same time, hear myself too." (2012, p. 51)

Cultivating silence while eliminating noise is a challenge to most individuals. Yet, it offers you the opportunity to hear yourself THINKing about the possibilities. Is high tech really hijacking high-touch? (Leider & Shapiro, 2012, p. 156) Whaley offers a chapter of whimsical stories of the symptoms of being *Prisoners of Technology*. (2006) One that stood out in my mind was: "If you work from home and find that you're still in your pajamas and haven't brushed you teeth, combed your hair, or taken a shower and it's 5:00 PM," then you're a prisoner of technology. THINK for a moment about your connectedness during the course of a day. Are you a prisoner?

Anne Lindbergh described the yearning for solitude in *Gifts from the Sea*. (Lindbergh, 1955, 1975, 1983, 2003) She crafts a story of sea shells that represent various aspects of her experiences at her sea side home. Her book framed her THINKing as to her way of living, her work-life balance, and the human interactions in which she engaged. She visualizes the oyster shell as her call to solitude amidst her return to the daily cadence of life to remind her that

> I must try to be alone for part of each year, even a week or a few days; and for part of each day, even for an hour or a few minutes in order to keep my core, my center, my island-quality. You will remind me that unless I keep the island-quality intact somewhere within me, I will have little to give my husband, my children, my friends or the world at large. You will remind me

that woman must be still as the axis of a wheel in the midst of her activities; that she must be the pioneer in achieving this stillness, not only for her own salvation, but for the salvation of family life, of society, perhaps even of our civilization. (Lindbergh, 2003)

Allen reminds us in As A Man Thinketh (1992) that

A man becomes calm in the measure that he understands himself as a thought-evolved being, for such knowledge necessitates the understanding of others as the result of thought, and as he develops a right understanding, and sees more and more clearly the internal relations of things by the action of cause and effect, he ceases to fuss and fume and worry and grieve, and remains poised, steadfast, serene.

The calm man, having learned how to govern himself, knows how to adapt himself to others; and they, in turn, reverence his spiritual strength, and feel that they can learn of him and rely upon him. The more tranquil a man becomes, the greater is his success, his influence, his power for good. Even the ordinary trader will find his business prosperity increase as he develops a greater self-control and equanimity, for people will always prefer to deal with a man whose demeanor is strongly equable.

The strong, calm man is always loved and revered. He is like a shade-giving tree in a thirsty land, or a sheltering rock in a storm. "Who does not love a tranquil heart, a sweet-tempered, balanced life? It does not matter whether it rains or shines, or what changes come to those possessing these blessings for they are always sweet, serene, and calm. That exquisite poise of character which we call serenity is the last lesson of culture; it is precious as wisdom, more to be desired than gold – yea, than even fine gold. How insignificant mere money-seeking looks in comparison with a serene life – a life that dwells in the ocean of Truth, beneath the waves, beyond the reach of tempests, in the Eternal Calm! (Allen, 1992)

In *Make Today Count*, John Maxwell (2004) recommends that time be spent daily THINKing. He further elaborates on eleven THINKing skills in *Thinking for a Change* that I found to be very insightful and would suggest further study to integrate into your talent assessment as an Encore Leader:

1. **Big picture thinking:** the ability to think beyond yourself and your world in order to process ideas with a holistic perspective
2. **Focused thinking:** the ability to think with clarity on issues by removing distractions and mental clutter from your mind
3. **Creative thinking:** the ability to break out of your "box" of limitations and explore ideas and options to experience a breakthrough
4. **Realistic thinking:** the ability to build a solid foundation on facts to think with certainty
5. **Strategic thinking:** the ability to implement plans that give direction for today and increase your potential for tomorrow
6. **Possibility thinking:** the ability to unleash your enthusiasm and hope to find solutions for even seemingly impossible situations
7. **Reflective thinking:** the ability to revisit the past in order to gain a true perspective and think with understanding
8. **Questioning popular thinking:** the ability to reject the limitations of common thinking and accomplish uncommon results
9. **Shared thinking:** the ability to include the heads of others to help you think "over your head" and achieve compounding results
10. **Unselfish thinking:** the ability to consider others and their journey to think with collaboration
11. **Bottom-line thinking:** the ability to focus on results and maximum return to reap the full potential of your thinking.

For greater success, Encore Leaders should assess their THINKing skills. Encore Leaders must utilize their natural THINKing skills and strengthen those that are weak by extending their network with associates or advisors who can offer different THINKing skills.

6. KNOWING YOUR "GOOD LIFE"

I struggled with understanding, advocating, and defining "good life." In Leider and Shapiro's book, *Repacking*, they define "The Good Life" as

> living in the place you belong, with the people you love, doing the right work, on purpose... the place where you live provides adequate opportunities for

you to do the kind of work you want to do. That your work gives you time to be with the people you really love. And that your deepest friendships contribute to the sense of community you feel in the place where you live and work. (Leider & Shapiro, 2012, p. 17)

With a clean sheet and the opportunity to plot your definition of the "good life," this mindset introduces the spirit of Encore Leadership. Knowing what defines your personal view of how you want to lead your life is critical to harnessing your time, talent and treasure to pursue that personal vision.

The Good Life Inventory offers an assessment of the key attributes of defining your "good life." (Leider & Shapiro, 2012, p. 40) Understanding what needs to be unpacked, the environment where you live, the people with whom you have relationships, clarity of purpose, and what then needs to be repacked provides a starting point for the Encore Leadership good life!

7. VALUING THE FREEDOM TO CHOOSE

"Experiences remind us that the freedom to choose is not something we have – and can therefore lose – but something we are. It is of our deepest essence, just waiting to be unpacked." (Leider & Shapiro, 2012, p. 7) Embarking upon the transition journey requires clarity around owning and controlling your time, talents, and treasures. The crux of transition is moving from a current state to a future state, which you design and find joyful fulfillment in life.

I distinctly recall a transition tipping point occurring in my life when I thought that I had lost the freedom to choose my professional path to success. When an IBM branch manager told me that a Black woman could not be successful as a sales representative in the Midwest, I felt as though he had self-declared the ownership of my destiny. I'd never been constrained by the limitations that others placed on me at that point in my life, and I was not ready to have him self-proclaim my destiny. Thus, denying my freedom to choose sales gave me the conviction to succeed in sales in the Midwest earning several IBM sales awards. So, THANKS to my naysayer. He gave me the strength to prove him wrong by succeeding in my choice of professions.

Shapiro (2012, p. 124) describes the choices he made in repacking as:

- Devoting less time to jobs for which I get paid, in order to allow myself time to do the work I need to for my own mental and emotional well-being.
- Making do with fewer "things" so as to have the experiences – educational and otherwise – that I want.
- Learning to say "no" to other people in order to say "yes" to myself.
- Deepening the existing relationships in my life, as opposed to widening my circle of new relationships.
- Finding beauty and satisfaction within, rather than always looking for the next "best thing" that's out there.
- Taking the long view, learning patience.

Johnson posits that "Your path is created by the choices you make." (2008, p. 60) With the concept of the life journey as a component of the Encore Leadership path, the freedom to determine your journey heightens the importance of this step. With your path being conceived of choices, it is important to choose wisely as choice impacts your brand identity. Success is dependent upon "a competitive difference, a consistent message, and a loyal audience." With beating the competition no longer a required competency as an Encore Leader, the freedom to choose a visionary direction is expansive.

Kloser reminds us to *"celebrate all of your freedoms today – the freedoms you experience where you live, and the freedoms you experience inside yourself as you grow and transform!"* (2012, p. 78)

ENCORE LEADERSHIP COMMUNITY (TGIFIACT)

The Global Institute for Innovative and Collaborative THINKing (TGIFiACT) is the community that has been established for the "courageous conversations" that individuals who are going through Encore Leadership transitions are invited to engage. Several purposes exist for the creation and engagement of this collaborative community. Having individuals in your network who listen to and communicate using the same language is often important during transition. This serves as a vehicle to build a trusted Encore Leadership community.

The desire for authentic human connections requires a higher quality of attention to one another with compassion that occurs when we genuinely listen, regardless of whether or not we agree. The challenge is to create genuine presence that supports positive change. (Leider & Shapiro, 2012, p. 113) TGIFiACT will endeavor to create spaces and networks for connections to manifest in reinvigorating communities of engagement that matter.

Frankl challenges transitioning individuals to find shared meaning in a new sense of community and common purpose in his exploration of *Man's Search for Ultimate Meaning*. (Frankl, 1963) His poignant story of life as a prisoner forces one to escape the mundane of comfort and to search for what truly matters in life. This classic story serves as a reminder of the need for community while adapting to the changing environmental challenges of daily life. Forced isolation versus choice isolation must be a constant and conscious choice for Encore Leaders.

Has technology truly hijacked the human moments in our lives? This question posed by Leider buttresses the debate of social isolation. He contends that as individuals become more connected via social media, disconnection occurs and more isolation is the result that undermines emotional well-being. Utilizing a proper mix of technology while creating physical connectedness will be the ongoing balancing act of TGIFiACT.

Storytelling will be a key component of courageous conversations, which are encouraged with TGIFiACT. Writing your story is a key exercise that will help to clarify your journey as an Encore Leader. Jim Loehr provides an 8-step process to storyboard your transformation. With detail scenarios painted in his book *The Power of Story* (Loehr, 2007), chapter twelve provides a workbook to develop your story. The provocative questions offer an opportunity to build and reflect upon the life that you are leading and choose to lead through telling your story. Shared examples include vision statements, mission statements, and stories that open dialogue for conversations to document your personal story.

Listening to the point of disappearing is a fundamental skill that must be adopted by Encore Leaders. Listening to discern information without being judgmental or leaping to conclusions and problem solving, when listening was the only request made. As we tell our stories, coaches and accountability partners must be ready to play back the tape, based on what they heard, to align with the voice and the heart of the speakers. This tough conversation will bring greater authenticity to storytellers and greater clarity to their work as Encore Leaders.

POIGNANT, PROVOCATIVE AND PIVOTAL QUESTIONS

"To unpack is to awaken; to see something different; to ask new questions. It is an expression of an urge to create, to live whole." (Leider & Shapiro, 2012, p. 18) As you consider cracking the transition code, THINK about and respond to these questions:

- **What's next?**
- **What's Your Definition of "The Good Life"?**
- **Are you living your "Good Life"?**
- **What needs to change or shift?**
- **What is the meaning of your life?**
- **What keeps you up at night vs. What wakes you up in the morning?**
- **What are your life's non-negotiables?**
- **How much is enough?**
- **What do you really want to carry on the next phase of your journey?**
- **Does all this make you happy?**
- **Where do you go for solitude?**
- **What are the lengths of time you engage in solitude?**
- **Are you living in your own big questions?**

"Life can never be adequately discussed or conceptualized, but only created – by living in our own questions, by continually unpacking and repacking our bags." (Leider & Shapiro, 2012, p. 20)

THE 4 PHASES AND THE 12 STEPS OF THE ENCORE LEADERSHIP PROCESS

After an individual hits the "Transition Tipping Point," 4 phases are identified as critical to reinventing life. They are:

1. **Re-Examine**
2. **Redefine**
3. **Reinvest**
4. **Reimagine**

As a math major with a high C behavior style, I prefer order in my THINKing and in my DOing. As I documented the Encore Leadership process, it was critical to establish guiding forces to follow that drive action. These forces are defined as:

DO… REFLECT… THINK… BE… ACT.

What should I DO to understand? Now, let me REFLECT on what I know. How do I THINK about this awareness? What will I BE as a result of my doing, reflecting, and THINKing? Now, ACT on my Being. You will experience these guiding forces in the process for each of the 12 steps.

In order to systematically approach transforming to Encore Leadership, I chose to organize the discoveries from the research and more than 10 years of coaching into buckets. These four buckets represent the phases that one traverses as he considers transforming his life. This approach helps to monitor and to clarify the stage of the process of reinvention that one may be experiencing.

By identifying the steps within the phases, I hope they will serve as a common roadmap for successful people to engage in the process. By you placing yourself in the process, it allows for a level of comfort in knowing that you are on the right path. It's like seeing a landmark on a map. If you continue far enough, you will discover the journey of Encore Leadership.

In summary, the four major phases of the Encore Leadership Process© are depicted in the following diagram along with the tipping point trigger.

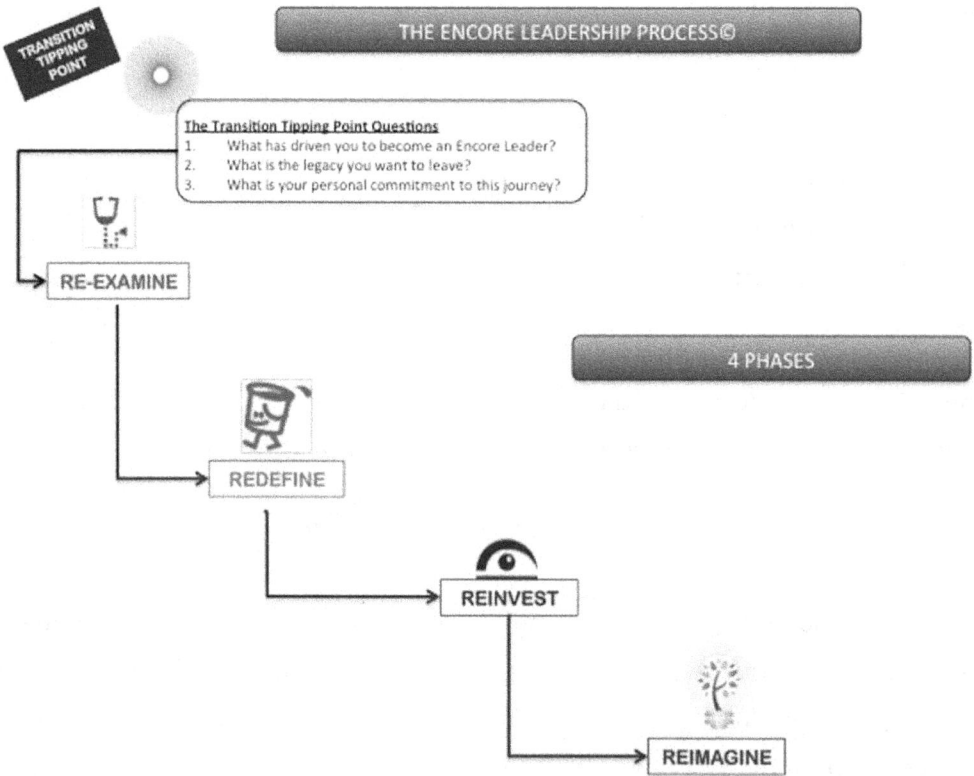

THE ENCORE LEADERSHIP PROCESS©

TRANSITION TIPPING POINT

The Transition Tipping Point Questions
1. What has driven you to become an Encore Leader?
2. What is the legacy you want to leave?
3. What is your personal commitment to this journey?

RE-EXAMINE

4 PHASES

REDEFINE

REINVEST

REIMAGINE

Figure 10. 4 Phases of the Encore Leadership Process©

There are 12 steps within the 4 phases that represent the areas of specific focus for Encore Leaders to move from successful to significant. The steps are not sequential, but it is important to clearly define each step for your personal journey.

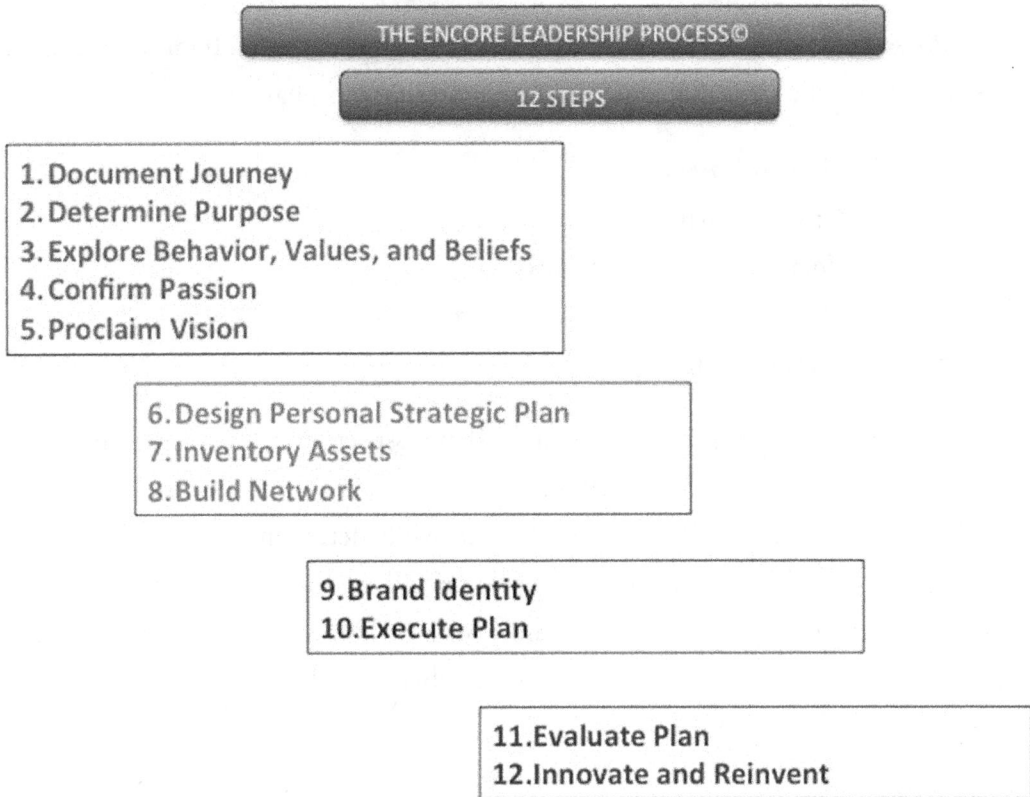

THE ENCORE LEADERSHIP PROCESS©

12 STEPS

1. Document Journey
2. Determine Purpose
3. Explore Behavior, Values, and Beliefs
4. Confirm Passion
5. Proclaim Vision

6. Design Personal Strategic Plan
7. Inventory Assets
8. Build Network

9. Brand Identity
10. Execute Plan

11. Evaluate Plan
12. Innovate and Reinvent

Figure 11. 12 Steps of the Encore Leadership Process©

I. RE-EXAMINE

"And be not conformed to this world: but be ye transformed by the renewing of your mind." Romans 12:2 (Felder, 2007)

Phase 1 of the Encore Leadership process is to re-examine your frame of references. There are five specific steps that are critical to mastering this phase of the process.

1.   **Document journey**
2.   **Determine purpose**
3.   **Explore behavior and values**
4.   **Confirm passion**
5.   **Proclaim vision**

Re-examination requires a great deal of introspection. The process allows for various tools to guide you through a self-assessment that will ground your transformation. It is important to celebrate past accomplishments while determining future aspirations. Often, the key to "what wakes you up" can be uncovered and fortified as a directional linkage to a next phase in life. This re-examination provides a means to compile the data that will be important to reflect upon as you deliberate with yourself and with others during this exploration phase.

Gaining clarity is also an objective of the re-examination phase. Being grounded in your perspective of the world will help attract the new experiences and opportunities that await you. Once this work has been done, you will be ready and convicted to the Encore Leadership vision for your life.

1. DOCUMENT JOURNEY

Celebrating your successful journey through life, thus far, is the first step in re-examining your life. Very seldom have we taken the time to really THINK about and applaud our personal accomplishments. When we hear our vitae or bio when we're being introduced at an event, it is often the singular time when we really THINK about our accomplishments. Therefore, documenting the journey is the first step in transforming into an Encore Leader.

THE TRANSITION JOURNEY EXERCISE

The "Transition Journey" exercise was created as a means to plot past successes, to highlight current areas of focus, and to begin to THINK about "what's next?" Taking the time to then look at the story that is told by the chart provides an initial roadmap to reflect upon the journey.

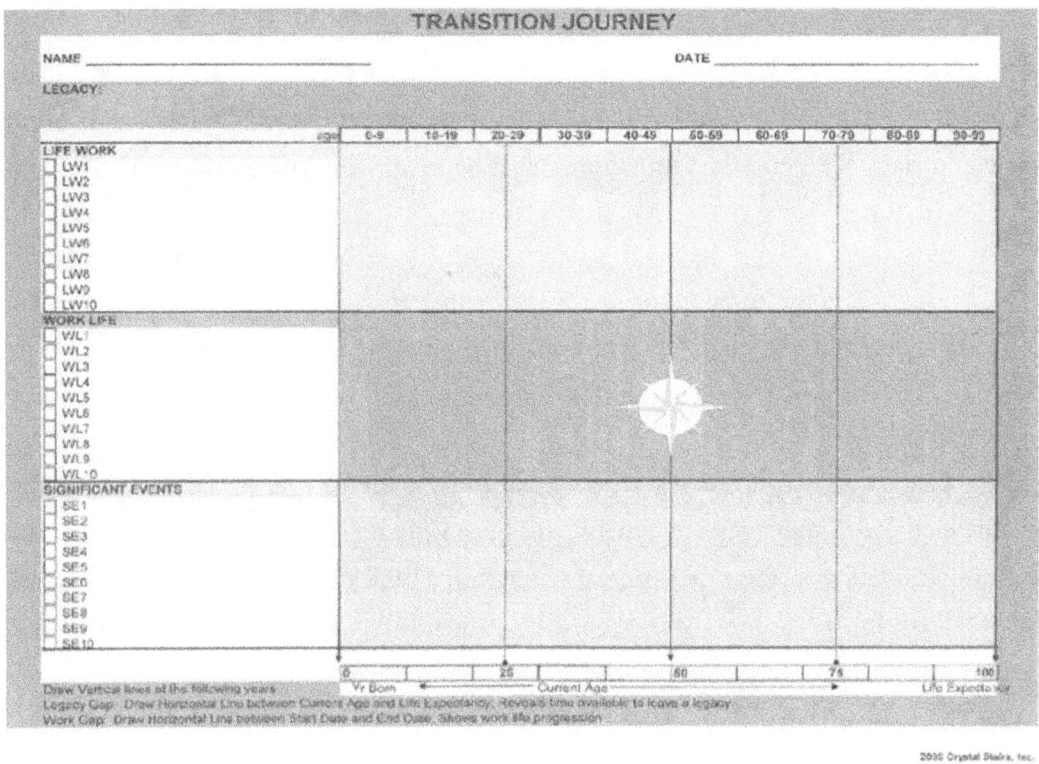

Figure 12. Transition Journey Exercise

Reinforcing the work associated with the past drives the need to ask the question, "Have I accomplished what I was placed on this earth to do?" What other questions does this exercise inspire?

FOUND

In the summer of 2013 after months of planning, my husband and I joined two friends on what we defined as 'the trip of a lifetime." Colette O'Brien, our travel agent with Alliance Travel in Atlanta, had taken care of every detail as we embarked upon this 19-day journey to South Africa, Botswana, Zambia and Kenya.

Preparing for the journey was challenging. From packing only 33-pounds to the series of immunizations required, it was quite the experience before even stepping onto the plane.

I read quite a few books and talked to several people who had traveled various segments of the trip, but I was most apprehensive about the four different safari camps we would visit. Well, not the camps as much as being up-close and personal with animals for more than ten days.

This was going to be quite an adventure into the unknown. I didn't know what to really expect but everyone had put their spin on their experience so I decided to be open to all of the possibilities and to live in the moment.

One morning prior to departure, I had coffee with my friend, Cathleen Wheatley, who helped me to quiet my anxiety. We discussed the book that had been on my mind and we wrestled with the title until we landed on FOUND. I wasn't sure what would be FOUND in Africa, but I was open to the adventure. Validating the direction, as I walked into church on the Sunday before departure, the organist was playing "Amazing Grace" with great fervor.

If you know the song, you recognize the power of being FOUND. I visited the bookstore on the Thursday before the Friday departure and FOUND a journal. The one that leaped out at me was titled, "Amazing Grace". My mother's favorite song… AMAZING GRACE.

The story of the journey to Africa will be captured in my book, FOUND: The Big 5 Game Changers of Life (Anticipated publication date: Fall, 2014). We FOUND the "Big 5" animals in all of our drives while on safari. The "Big 5" denotes the 5 most aggressive animals to hunt. The incredible journey to Africa was only the beginning of a lifetime of reflection and stories that penetrated our souls, our hearts and our minds. Stay tuned for the book, FOUND.

In the meantime, I would challenge every Encore Leader to THINK about the top 5 things that could possibly change the trajectory of your life.

What are the Big 5 Game Changers for your life?

1. _____

2. _____

3. _____

4. _____

5. _____

LIFE LINE

The Information Technology Senior Management Forum (ITSMF) organization exposed me to a wonderful technique to prepare, reflect, and share my life's story. The process, affectionately called a "Life Line," of preparing a PowerPoint presentation on the highlights and challenges of your life provides an opportunity to "talk out loud" about your personal journey.

For many, it opens up a past that has been purposefully left behind that might inform your future when you take the time to understand "how you got over!" Further, it often serves as a means for others to compare their world and to understand that roadblocks can be successfully navigated.

Often, when one honestly tells her story, she gives a gift to someone who may be struggling with the same or a similar issue. Creating forums and opportunities to share from the heart "from whence one has come" often is the trigger for someone's success.

Include in your "Life Line" a sequencing of the following categories accompanied with pictures, artifacts, or other memorabilia that visually portray your story in a slideshow presentation.

1.   Parents and Guardians; Family History
2.   Your Birth
3.   Your Siblings or other key family members
4.   Your Early Childhood (Influencers: Teachers, geography, Family members, mentors, etc.)
5.   Your Middle School and High School Years
6.   Your College Years and Post-Graduate Work
7.   First Job, Job History (Mentors, sponsors, situations, assignments, geography)
8.   Marriage, Your Family, Other dynamics of relationships
9.   Your religious journey
10. Things and situations that you think influenced your "being"
11. What you enjoy doing for fun and leisure
12. People who you admire

Add music to slides from each point in time referenced. Add some family and/or national history to position the moment. Share your "Life Line" with family, associates, and colleagues. Have Fun!

BUCKET LIST

We have heard a lot of discussion regarding "bucket lists" subsequent to the focus of several movies with senior characters determining what they want to do before they die. Also, the book *1,000 Places To See Before You Die: A Traveler's Life List* (Schultz, 2003) continues to popularize the notion of creating a bucket list. Yet, not many people take the time to really document their list of items that they want to "do" in life.

THINKing about this idea and documenting a list is the first step in planning your personal list of "to-dos" while encouraging others to share the journey with you. It provides a means for anticipation of "great adventures" while establishing a sense of future goals and objectives. It provides an energy plan as critical as the career plan that many of us plotted in answering the question, what do you want to be when you grow up?

In particular, I often find that reading others' "bucket lists" stretches my THINKing to help me focus on my own set of future objectives. I provide one such bucket list in my workbook, available at www.EncoreLeadership.com, if you need a trigger to get your THINKing started. Just ask yourself, what have I always wanted to do, but haven't done? Then, DO IT!

Also, visit EncoreLeadership.org and blog your thoughts or read the thoughts of others who are navigating through this journey of reinvention.

Noted author and speaker Brian Tracy shared the following reflection as a motivational thought to navigating the transition journey:

> You are unique in every sense. There is no one in the world, in all of human history, with the special combination of talents, abilities, knowledge, experience, insights, feelings, desires, ambitions, hopes, or dreams that you have. And there never will be.

> Your greatest satisfaction and joy in life will come when you have the wonderful feeling that you are realizing your full potential and becoming everything you are capable of becoming. (Tracy, 2009, p. 11)

A LEGACY THAT MATTERS

Melissa Johnson believes that "Legacy is the unique opportunity to make an impact for years to come" and that "The essence of legacy is that your life is so full that you are able to pass a portion to someone else." (2008, pp. 142, 145) She further offers to live your legacy today by following three steps:

1. Commit to Grow – Be open to improvement.
2. Commit to Give Back – Share the best of who you are with others.
3. Commit to Write – Expound upon your life through the written word.

These three principles are embedded in the work of The Global Institute for Innovative and Collaborative THINKing (TGIFiACT). For Encore Leaders, leaving a legacy that matters is a primary area of focus for transforming life from successful to significant. As one becomes more conscious of the inevitable process of the circle of life, one acknowledges that legacy is important.

At lunch with my dear friend Carter Womack, he very definitively stated as he talked about another friend with a terminal illness that "we are all terminal." Clarity. FOCUS. A legacy that matters.

2. DETERMINE PURPOSE

The search for purpose is an ongoing journey that individuals embark upon. Often, asking the question, what is my purpose on this earth?, is the step in the Encore Leadership process that invites the challenging work of determining purpose. James Allen shares in his book, *As A Man Thinketh*:

> A man should conceive of a legitimate purpose in his heart, and set out to accomplish it. He should make this purpose the centralizing point of his thoughts. It may take the form of a spiritual ideal, or it may be a worldly object, according to his nature at the time being; but whichever it is, he should steadily focus his thought forces upon the object which he has set before him. He should make this purpose his supreme duty, and should devote himself to its attainment, not allowing his thoughts to wander away into ephemeral fancies, longings, and imaginings. This is the royal road to self-control and true concentration of thought. Even if he fails again and again to accomplish his purpose (as he necessarily must until weakness is overcome), the strength of character gained will be the measure of his true success, and this will form a new starting point for future power and triumph. (Allen, 1992)

"It's vital to become clear about our life's purpose so that we can carry what we're carrying with balance, fortitude, and joy…What most of us, what we're really looking for is a feeling – a feeling of aliveness." (Leider & Shapiro, 2012, p. 7) "The thread that holds the good life together is purpose. Defining your sense of purpose – your thread – enables you to continually travel in the direction of your vision of the good life. It keeps you focused on where you want to go and discovering new roads to get there." (Leider & Shapiro, 2012, p. 17)

A guiding thought as I decided how to frame "purpose" was the insight provided by Kloser that *"As you fulfill your personal purpose, you are contributing one more piece to the entirety of all life."* (2012, p. 31) The notion of mattering as evidenced in research connects the importance of purpose for Encore Leaders. (Foster, 2009)

Several tools and thought provokers are included in this section. They include:

1. Life Purpose Worksheet
2. Purpose Literature

LIFE PURPOSE WORKSHEET

LIFE PURPOSE WORKSHEET

Why are you alive?	
What are you most proud of having accomplished at this point in your life?	
If you were financially able to retire one year from today, what would you begin working on to prepare for that?	
What would you most like the people at your funeral to say about you, specifically?	
Who in history do you admire most, and why?	
If you could solve a world problem, what would it be? Be VERY specific please.	
What is the inkling you have of your purpose or vision?	
What is in the way of putting this ahead of what you are engaged in now?	
If it weren't important to have a life purpose, what would you most like to do in the next decade?	
List 3 possible life purposes.	1. 2. 3.

Form courtesy of and copyrighted by Coach U, Inc.; ©2001, coachville.com

Figure 13. Life Purpose Worksheet

PURPOSE LITERATURE

There have been several authors who have shared expert knowledge regarding "purpose." The following are books related to purpose that are highlighted in this section:

- *The Purpose Driven Life*
- *Fulfilled*
- *Pebbles in the Pond, Wave Two*
- *Halftime*
- *Claiming Your Place at the Fire*
- *The Power of Purpose: Find Meaning, Live Longer*
- *The 7 Mindsets to Live Your Ultimate Life*
- *The Eight Cylinders of Success*

The Purpose Driven Life by Rick Warren (2002) is a 40-day process to explore your purpose. The popular book, journal, meditations, and daily inspiration are resources that provide a disciplined approach to ascertaining your purpose. Warren masterfully weaves an understanding of purpose with his acronym, SHAPE: spiritual gifts, heart, abilities, personality, and experiences. He suggests that knowing these elements of your being will help you discover your ministry to the world. He further states that "you have to choose whom you can best help, based on your shape." (2002)

Fulfilled (Martin, 2002, 2009) provides eight key principles to navigate in seeking balance and fulfillment in life. Jacquie Martin's directive is that one should take "responsibility, own and embrace all of your experiences in order to fully appreciate and comprehend how your life is and has been shaped." Her eight principles are:

1. The Law of Perception
2. The Law of Promise
3. The Law of Thanksgiving
4. The Law of Commitment
5. The Law of Harmony
6. The Law of Readiness
7. The Law of Creativity
8. The Law of Empowerment

Pebbles in the Pond, Wave Two (Kloser, 2013) shares the experience of many authors who have discovered their purpose. This chapter books offers personal stories of tests that enabled testimonies. Kloser's own affirmation speaks to the truth of finding purpose:

Help Me Be…

Strong enough to be vulnerable.

Wise enough to realize how little I know.

Loving enough to embrace my "enemy."

Tender enough to be powerful.

Smart enough to realize I can't do it alone.

Brilliant enough to shine the light of others.

Doubtful enough to know the power of faith.

Courageous enough to share my truth.

Halftime is one of many books that Bob Buford has authored. (2000) While the books in and of themselves are thought provoking, I discovered his work in a manner that continues to validate my work and to attract the insight necessary to explore and discover your purpose. While on vacation in California, as I was walking back to my room from the spa, I held a brief conversation with a gentleman who was wearing a nametag that showed he was a participant in a conference. The discussion led me to understand that the conference was a gathering of individuals who were working on their "halftime." No coincidences!

In *Claiming Your Place at the Fire*, Leider and Shapiro profoundly articulate the rationale for purpose as a major consideration of reinventing life.

The reason why the issue of purpose is so important to a vital second half of life is that it raises issues that, ultimately, are inevitable. None of us is going to get out of this life without facing the question "Why am I here?" None of us is going to be able to avoid confronting the question of our life's meaning. We don't really get away with not wondering what our legacy will be after we're gone.

By thinking intentionally about our life's purpose – by thoughtfully reflecting on our life's meaning – we give ourselves the time and space to think about things that sooner or later we're going to have to think about, whether we want to or not. And if we do this well and do it with intention, we can define our life's purpose and reclaim it so that we are able to integrate it successfully in all that we do throughout the second half of our lives. New elders do this and do so in ways that make their lives more vital for themselves and for family, friends, and, in many cases, clients and customers as well. (Leider and Shapiro, 2004, p. 113)

Leider and Shapiro offer four major considerations for reclaiming your place:

1. The Flame of Identity: Recalling Our Stories
2. The Flame of Community: Refinding Our Place
3. The Flame of Passion: Renewing Our Calling
4. The Flame of Meaning: Reclaiming Our Purpose

Dialogues by Encore Leaders, who are exploring their Encore Leadership lives, are well served in reviewing this "reclaiming" framework as they take the stage at the top of the leadership maturation life cycle and their seat around the fire. Instructive in exploring life at all stages is the Life Spiral developed by Leider and discussed in *The Power of Purpose*. (2010, p. 142)

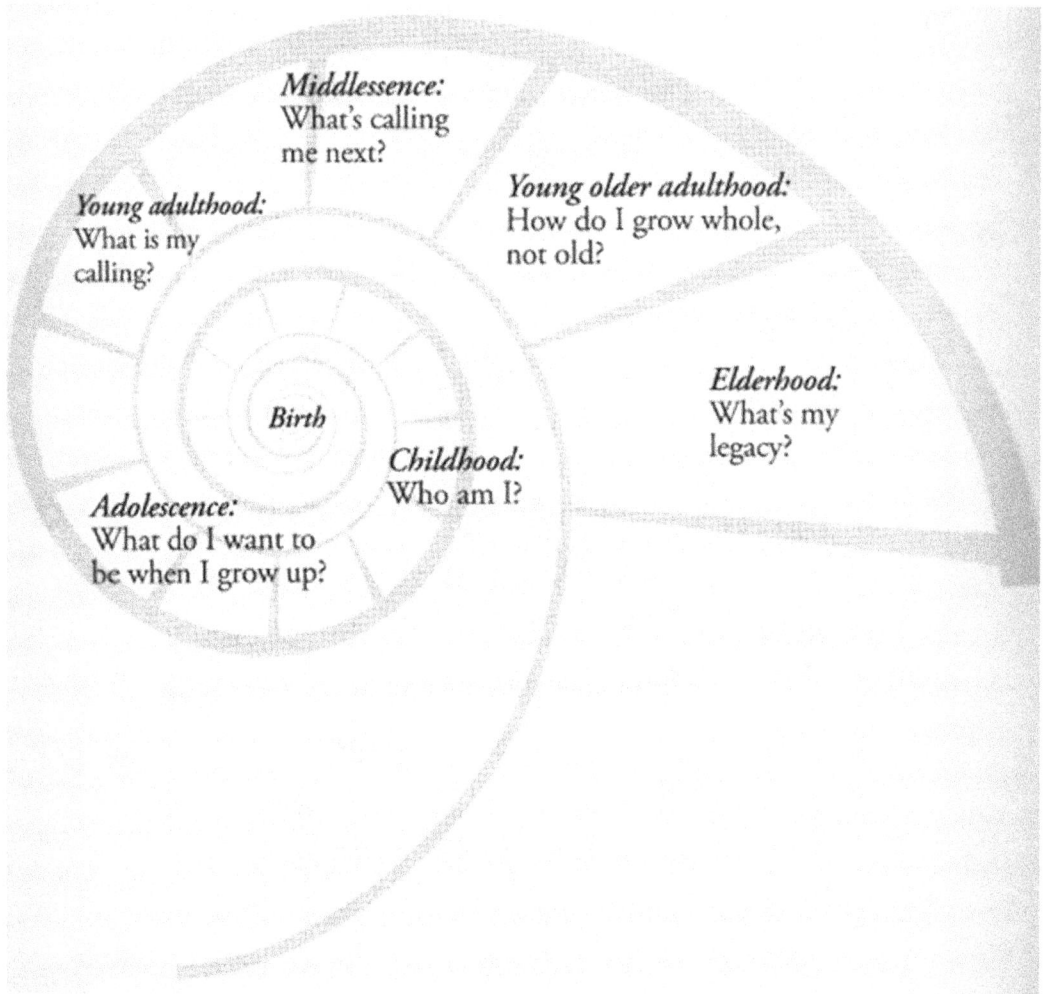

Figure 14. The Life Spiral

Use the illustration to map out your "life spiral" with meaningful and specific events throughout your journey!

Elder Circles, advocated by Ram Dass, (Leider & Shapiro, 2004, p. 6) served as the foundation for the objective to connect Encore Leaders with Legacy Voices. Legacy Voices are children, protégés and/or high-potential talent who are connected to Encore Leaders. Sharing lives that are purpose driven across generations provides a strong impetus for engagement in legacy work that matters. In particular, sharing knowledge derived from the different environments that change over time accommodates the wisdom sharing that is both contemporary and traditional THINKing based on experience and longevity of life.

The 7 Mindsets To Live Your Ultimate Life: An unexpected blueprint for an extraordinary life (Shickler, 2011) provides a provocative dialogue that can be embraced as a roadmap to a life of meaning. Geared toward young people, the mindsets were compiled through interviews to determine the ones that successful people have in common. They offer a benchmark for THINKing as Encore Leaders. The mindsets are:

1. Everything is Possible
2. Passion First
3. We are Connected
4. 100% Accountable
5. Attitude of Gratitude
6. Live to Give
7. The Time is Now

These seven mindsets serve as continued validation when integrated into the Encore Leadership process when successful people opt to do work that matters and to leave a legacy of mattering.

The 8 Cylinders of Success discusses how to align your personal and professional purpose. (Gordon, 2009) Paramount to the insight that is provided by Gordon is the notion of eight effects of purpose. While Encore Leaders are looking in the rear view mirror and mapping their success to the opportunities they were afforded, Legacy Voices are instructed on the impact of their future choices. These eight effects that are related to purpose are:

1. Education
2. Employment
3. Environment
4. Emotions
5. Energy

6. Earnings
7. Experiences
8. Entourage

Gordon further offers "5 Points on the Path of Purpose." This guidance is applicable to the shift required when one is considering transforming himself, whether as an Encore Leader or a Legacy Voice. The points are:

1. Inquiring: Starting to question it
2. Investigating: Starting to explore it
3. Invoking: Starting to voice it to others
4. Investing: Starting to put energy into it (e.g., time & money)
5. Inspiring: Starting to inspire others with it

Gordon contends that if you are not working on one of the points, you may need to assess if you are off the path of purpose or "indifferent." Where are you on the path of purpose?

3. EXPLORE BEHAVIOR, VALUES AND BELIEFS

Understanding our own invisible drivers can literally change our lives by giving us more conscious choices over the decisions we make. – Judy Suiter

Understanding and aligning "self" is a major milestone in the Encore Leadership process. Identifying your behavior style, values, and beliefs provides a foundation for exploring your Encore Leadership life. Your behavior style will tell you what your preferred way of doing things tends to be while your values will tell you why you most often do the things that you do. "Values can affect a person's behavioral style by either softening some styles or magnifying others." (Suiter, 2003, p. 54)

BEHAVIOR

"Many people are laboring through their lives, weighed down by attachments that no longer serve them. Patterns of behavior that have helped them get where they are, aren't helping them get where they want to be." (Leider & Shapiro, 2012, p. 6) The behavior shift required to crack the transition code is paramount to Encore Leadership. Research has provided an assessment of the shifts that include:

- From concern for career growth to concern for form or creative expression and personal growth;
- From beating competition to community consciousness;
- From concern for competence to inner peace and self care.

I was exposed to the importance of understanding one's dominant behavior style when I was training for my coaching certificate. Subsequently, I was certified in the DiSC® Behavior Style training and I have assessed thousands of people and organizations since that time. I have found that when a person can discern the appropriate behavior to invoke in a given situation and environment as a result of aligning his personal behavior with the behavior style of others, a more productive dialogue and engagement can ensue. The conscious and intentional shifting of behavior is a skill that can be mastered as one integrates this understanding to her day-to-day interactions.

I experienced behavior shifts during my personal transitions. While I still remain very conscientious about my approach to life, I use the shift of my influence behavior style more extensively as I re-create my brand. I also find that I have less need to be dominant and attempt to drive more toward steadiness. However, with performance at the root of my being, my conscientious style remains a preference for my behavior. I always seek to do better than my best!

In my book, *Due North! Strengthen Your Leadership Assets* (Foster, 2002), I included behavior as one of twelve traits that successful leaders must master. Examples of how behavior "plays out" becomes a recognizable aspect of gaining success in professional relationships and on teams.

In *Energizing People*, Suiter notes that "people are different in their [behavior] preferences, their viewpoints, and their behaviors. This statement does not presume that differing behavioral styles are good or bad, better or worse – they are simply different from each other. The way we see and respond to various situations identifies our behavioral styles." (2003)

VALUES

"Our true value is more than what we do, how much we make, or how many things we own – it's simply who we are". (Leider & Shapiro, 2012, p. 180)

Establishing a value-based personal life system is a critical milestone in determining the journey to Encore Leadership. There are two primary instruments that I have found to be helpful during the transition from first career to second pursuits to become values grounded. The Life Compass® (see Figure 15) and The Personal Interests, Attitudes, and Values Assessment provide great insight on values.

THE LIFE COMPASS

It is often beneficial to take the temperature of what is most critical or important in your life at any given time. The Life Compass® exercise (see Figure 15) allows one to level set her priorities while making distinctions at any given time when balance is required in decision-making. A compass provides a visible reminder to manage all of the various components of life.

FAMILY

EXTREME
SELF-CARE

N

FRIENDS

HOBBIES/
FUN

NETWORK

FINANCIAL

SOCIAL/
RELATIONSHIPS

PROFESSION

HEALTH

INTELLECT

ENVIRONMENT

SPIRITUAL

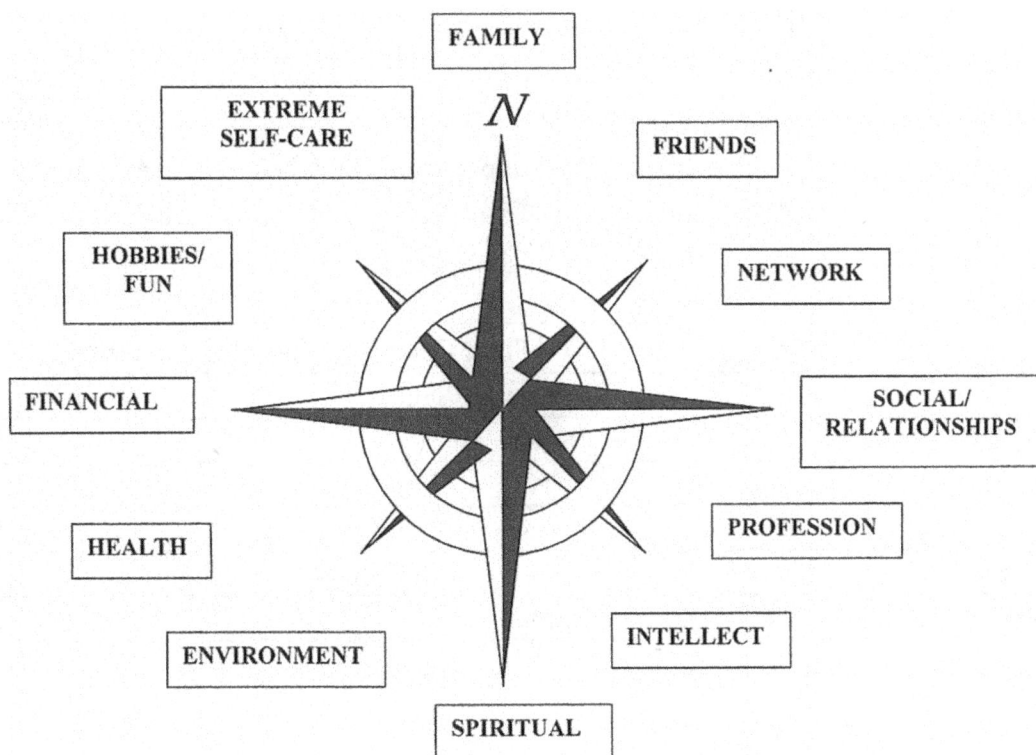

CRYSTAL STAIRS LIFE COMPASS©

A plan to live a meaningful life requires taking a look at where you are today relative to where you want to be in any given aspect of your life.

For each area of your life, assess where you are currently on a scale of 0–10. (0 is the bull's-eye of the circle, no place; 10 is the best it could be, the outer circle perimeter.) Place a dot between 0 and 10 to indicate where you are today. Then connect the dots to find the balance of your compass, your life. Review each and put a dot where you would like to be in the element and connect those dots.

The space in between the dots represents the "gap" that you want to bridge. Prioritize the three largest gaps and take three immediate actions this week to address each of the three. Include a detailed plan as a component of your "journey assessment."

Figure 15. Crystal Stairs Life Compass©

THE PERSONAL INTERESTS, ATTITUDES AND VALUES (PIAV) ASSESSMENT

Exploring Values! Releasing the Power of Attitudes (Suiter, 2003) provides an explanation of value motivators that are classified into clusters. These six clusters include: Theoretical, Utilitarian, Aesthetic, Social, Individualistic, and Traditional. Each of these clusters is a factor in the determinants of what motivates an individual.

In the research methodology for the Cracking the Transition Code Dissertation, (Foster, 2009) (see Part I of this book) a survey was conducted in which questions were asked to assess any shift in values based on the Personal Interests, Attitudes and Values (PIAV) assessment clusters as factors. The comparative analysis of questions #30 and #50 in the survey discovered a statistically significant shift in how values were ranked from first career to second pursuits. The PIAV analysis revealed the following data:

Values	First Career to Second Pursuits
Theoretical	#3 Positive Shift
Utilitarian	Neutral
Aesthetic	#2 Positive Shift
Social	#1 Positive Shift
Individualistic	Only Negative Shift
Traditional	Neutral

Figure 16. Personal Interests, Attitudes and Values

This data reflected a need to consciously assess and define the value system of individuals as they transition to a transformed Encore Leadership life. Determining the importance of the potential values shift, the rationale for it, or examples that are presented, fortify this component of the journey. To specifically understand where your current set of values stack up with these clusters, the Personal Interests, Attitudes, and Values Assessment is a great tool to gain specific insight.

Behavioral styles that were discussed in step three of the Encore Leadership process "measure *how* a person does things; values tells *why* they do the things they do." With that distinction in mind, individuals tend to do things as categorized in six different value clusters:

Theoretical – love ideas and exploring new interests.   Enjoy accumulating knowledge resulting in traits of greater sense of objectivity, sharper critical THINKing skills, and the ability to debate on a more rational level. Low knowledge seekers tend to learn on demand or when needed.

Engagement suggestions for Encore Leaders with high theoretical value style:

1. Additional education; classes to learn new skills;
2. Reading more;
3. Searching the Internet and experimenting with new tools;
4. Doing work that has always been intriguing – corporate sales to actor; marketing executive to artist; accountant to sculptor.

New interests could lead to a million pathways. The key is to be open and to not allow the social cluster or the utilitarian attitude to seep into the exploration of new ideas and interests.

Utilitarian – desire for wealth and expected return on investment for time, energy, and money. The dichotomy of the value is that people with a high utilitarian value are also fiscally conservative. They choose to amass wealth rather than spend it on extravagances. Success and happiness are not measured by financial gain, per the architect of the world wide web who made no financial gain from the work. (Suiter, 2003, p. 28) The web was built to support and advocate for the open and free access for all to information.

Engagement suggestions for Encore Leaders with high utilitarian value style:

1. Passionately advocating for a cause;
2. Philanthropic endeavors;
3. Creating a foundation.

Aesthetic – Concern for form and function, e.g., harmony in relationships, thirst for personal growth, and creative expression. This value is exemplified throughout Issacson's book on Steve Jobs. (Isaacson, 2011) Jobs' uncompromising spirit of beauty was a major driving force throughout his life. He consistently and constantly challenged design and studied design from an aesthetic frame of reference.

Suiter shares a story in her book that is particularly relevant to this discussion.

Catherine Carlisi's mother, Kay, exemplifies the *Aesthetic* sensibility in her desire for harmony in relationships, beautiful surroundings, and a thirst for personal growth and creative expression that has kept her enthusiastic and vibrant when others her age have grown bitter and discontented. Kay tends to view events with a true *Aesthetic* point-of-view. She has dabbed in painting, music, and home decorating, and she awakens each day with a sense of anticipation about what life experiences await her. In fact, Kay is something of a legend in the local golf club, where infighting and gossip were the norm before she threatened to quit her position as club president unless harmony was restored. "Life is too short for pettiness," she told them. "Count your blessings and enjoy each day." Kay also holds the record for eliciting the most hugs in a single day during the fellowship hour at her church. (Suiter, 2003, pp. 30-31)

Suiter further reveals:

Dreamers, artists, poets, inventors, philosophers, and other creative individuals are often guided by a strong *Aesthetic* values cluster from their early years, while others may "graduate" to *Aesthetic* motivations later in life, after satisfying other driving passions. For example, many of the industrial magnates of the last century became famous as philanthropists in their later years contributing much to the beauty and art that we now enjoy in municipal parks, museums and other institutions they funded. (Suiter, 2003, p. 31)

The possibilities to extend the interests of people with aesthetic interests is validated by the finding that the aesthetic value cluster is the second greatest positive shift experienced by individuals seeking to transform their lives.

Engagement suggestions for Encore Leaders with high aesthetic value style:

1.   Take a calligraphy class; Steve Jobs used his calligraphy class experience as the foundation for fonts on Macintosh computers (Macs). I took a calligraphy class at 57 years of age, on a whim, at a bookstore and found it to be an amazing afternoon of exploring the art of calming the self by invoking the spirit of art;

2. Take a painting class at a local creative venue;
3. Visit a local art museum; Adopt and sponsor an artist's work; Become a docent;
4. Take a course in decorating or interior design.

Social – Community consciousness, volunteers, serves others. This value cluster was rated as the number one shift that was experienced by transitioning executives. While providing community service through leadership and/or some personal involvement while in the first career, this value cluster became more pronounced in the second pursuits. Sacrificing their own needs for others is a trait that is represented by individuals with high social values. However, utilitarian and individualistic values may soften the depth of this values cluster. More engagement with human rights advocacy and eliminating major challenges in the world through projects like:

- Habitat for Humanity;
- The 100 Black Men, Men of Tomorrow Mentoring Program;
- Big Brother and Big Sisters;
- Teach For America sponsorship;
- Inroads support of students;
- Make a Wish Foundation;
- The Jackie Robinson Foundation support;
- Sorority and Fraternity Youth group support and participation such as the Zeta Pearlettes, Amicettes and Archonettes.

These are a few organizations where Encore Leaders are giving back with the Social Cluster Value at the core of their transformed life. With which organizations are you involved where working with youth and/or helping others drives your energy?

Martin Luther King, Jr. is a prominent reminder of a focus on the Social Value Cluster. Further, his teaching of non-violence and helping others was very prominent in his words and deeds. Adopting this value as a component of one's life purpose is indicative of the strong focus on this cluster in a second pursuit of transformed individuals.

Engagement suggestions for Encore Leaders with high social value style:

1. Get involved in an organization where your expertise can be utilized;
2. Support a non-profit youth organization;
3. Add social engagement in your current organization and lead the effort.

Individualistic – Beating competition, rising to the top, winner and power. It is important to assess this value cluster because it is the only one that resulted in a negative shift in the transition survey. The respondents found that their desire for individualistic patterns declined from first career to second pursuit. The desire for beating competition and fighting to reach the top of the ladder declined considerably. Yet, it is important to match the other values to this value cluster. Examples of combining the high individualistic value style with other value styles include:

1. High individualistic value and high social — may be a strong anonymous donor;
2. High individualistic and high traditional — may be steered toward motivational speaking;
3. High individualistic and high aesthetic value — Suiter shares that Frank Lloyd Wright stated under oath:

I'm Frank Lloyd Wright, and I'm the greatest architect who ever lived. I have to state that because I am under oath. (Suiter, 2003, p. 44)

Another example of this combination of values clusters is Steve Jobs, who infamously believed that products should be designed with great attention to their aesthetic view. While focused on the utilitarian profitability of his company and the tradeoffs inherent in the development of products, he was a strong supporter of optimizing product design to take into account the aesthetic beauty of the work, as taught to him by his father. (Isaacson, 2011)

Engagement suggestions for Encore Leaders with high individualistic value style:

1. Engage in a sport for the enjoyment of the exercise;
2. Shift THINKing from being to supporting; Lead Actor role to Supporting Actor;
3. Serve on Boards and in organizations in a non-presidential/non-chair leadership role and mentor the next generation of leaders;
4. Ask questions as opposed to telling stories; Focus on others and not on self.

Traditional – Living by a set of rules and encouraging others to accept the same or similar standards or attitudes. This cluster experienced no significant shift in the transition survey. This value encompasses the desire to live within a set of rules. Often, religious view points or other endeavors, where individuals accept the same set of standards, is noted as the traditional values cluster. Principle-based convictions often find these individuals taking a strong stand or position on a subject. Billy Graham is noted as a strong tradition-based value example. Ideologies set the foundation for this value and are often at conflict with those who may not be as adaptable to shifting the traditional values cluster.

Engagement suggestions for Encore Leaders with high traditional value style:

1. Document the beliefs that you hold true with an unwavering approach and/or conviction;
2. Establish the Biblical guidelines or other foundation for how you will live your life;
3. Evaluate your historical journey and what traditions you uphold in your family or other circles of life.

BELIEFS

Understanding the values clusters allows one to creatively paint a picture of values using the "Beliefs and Values" circles developed by Curvie Burton. He has practiced the review of his "circles" and translated the process into a "dialogue around core beliefs and values." His focus on reassessing his priorities is depicted in the graphic of his "circles."

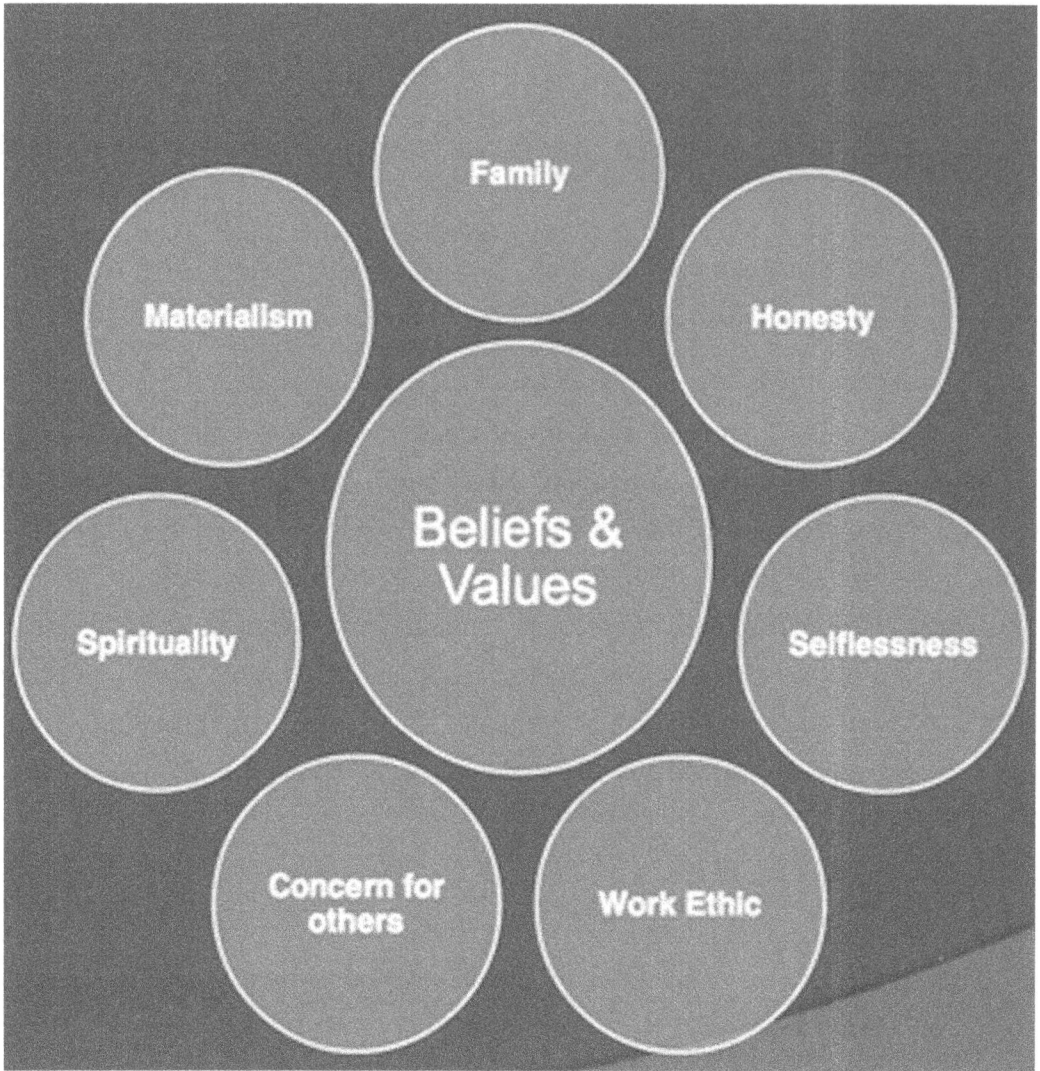

Figure 17. Beliefs and Values Diagram

Aligning and adjusting each of the circles on a regular basis maintains an appropriate focus and priority of all the dynamics of life as they rotate and are tossed around. This graphical depiction can serve as a method to inspect the singular as well as the interconnectedness of the circles at any given time in life.

There are two Encore Leadership concepts to embrace that require personal introspection and a personal belief system. Spirituality and the law of attraction are fundamental building blocks that one should explore.

Dale Bourke contends in her book, *Second Calling: Finding Passion & Purpose for the rest of your life*, that the foundation of our second calling is prayer. (2006) Her example of Naomi from the Book of Ruth sets the stage for her belief system. She believes that prayer is "a calling in itself, as well as the way in which we will find our path through the second half of life." Her very strong belief causes Encore Leaders to assess the spiritual component of their Encore Leadership life to ensure a firm foundation has been established in this competency.

Testimony about spirituality from Encore Leader Angela Brown touched my heart as she reflected in a Facebook posting. Angela and Johnny were college friends who became husband and wife. They were inseparable in college and in life.

It has been exactly one month since my husband left this world. People ask how I'm doing and I say "getting better every day". What I want to say is "I have a serious case of MMOM (Missing My Old Man)."

I smile at jokes that only he would appreciate; I look for him to walk into a crowded room; I see him in our sons as they walk, talk or when I look at their profiles. And yes, I still feel him close, when he'd sneak up, whisper in my ear, pat my bottom or give me one of those "I'll see you later" laughs.

Let me be fair, because of my faith, I know I'm getting better each day. Because of my wonderful family, I am not alone or feel unloved. Because of a wide circle of friends and associates, I have been showered with great love, affection, prayers and so many acts of kindness. I am busy because unexpected death has lots of business matters that must be addressed (you have no idea). As I go through his things, I found stuff that was kept for reasons no one else understands; I found his report cards, certificates from grade school and pictures of me that I had long forgotten. When I found packs of cigarettes and lighters, I became angry with me because maybe if I had thrown them away earlier or forbidden him to smoke in the house, he'd still be here with me (Nah). At these moments, I remember that this is a normal part of the grieving process. And only God can deal with the "would haves, should haves and the whys". I am at peace.

In my quiet times, I hear the Holy Spirit teaching me about the "New Normal", not the show, but for this phase of life. Last Sunday, when I returned to the pulpit, I preached from Mark 13. Jesus was asked by the disciples to explain the "things that will happen and when the end will come". Jesus says in verse 32," No man knows the day or the hour." He tells them to watch and pray; no one knows when the master will come back. This time that we're in when economies, governments, communities, ministries, leaders and family support systems that we relied on, are crumbling all around us is the new normal. But there are instructions for overcoming even the most difficult times of the "New Normal"

Here's what I'm learning through my new normal:

1) Recognize: Ain't nothing normal about the new normal (Don't get stuck here)

2) Acknowledge: There are some things we must endure to overcome; Don't be deceived

3) Accept: No matter what, our God has already begun an intervention to rescue you; Don't be discouraged

4) Process: Watch for the change God is bringing through you, because the world is watching you as you endure; how you endure what you're going through is where God can get the glory

5) Pray: Pray always as you go through what is your "new normal"; Pray without ceasing as you go through this new phase of life; Pray for the Master is returning; Pray and remain confident that God will receive the victory through you and for you.

God Bless.
Pastor Angela Brown
Charity A.M.E. Zion Church
Baltimore, MD

The *Law of Attraction* (Losier, 2003, 2006) offers a 3-step formula for deliberately attracting that which you desire.

1. Identify Your Desire
2. Give Your Desire Attention
3. Allow It

When you THINK about karma, luck, coincidence, fate and other descriptors for the law of attraction, consider making a conscious and intentional goal to attract what you desire in your Encore Leadership life.

4. CONFIRM PASSION

"Passion is the pulse behind your purpose." (Johnson, 2008, p. 47)

What causes your energy level to accelerate when you are discussing something with a friend? Often, passion is the cause. You have an affinity for the work or a cause that becomes your passion. What do people observe you to be passionate about? What do you want to engage in as a movement? What do you REALLY care about?

In climbing Mt. Everest, Jamie Clarke and Alan Hobson discovered the power of passion. They observed that "two very different people can achieve new heights if they share a common goal and a burning desire to work towards it, no matter what the obstacles." (Hobson, 1997) Their journey highlights the strength of passion when applied to a purpose-driven mission.

A major driver of passion is maintaining a positive mental attitude. A pre-cursor to attitude requires several exercises of eliminating things that you are tolerating; letting go of old baggage; attacking fear, uncertainty, and doubt with faith; and conducting a clean sweep of life. There are exercises that provide tools to engage in each of these activities included in the Encore Leadership Workbook, available through EncoreLeadership.com. (Tearte, 2013)

My sister, Maxine, has always had a gift of creative vision in working with crafts. She expresses her talent by investing her time creating unique sorority paraphernalia. Her signature items have fueled her ability to provide treasures that are valued by sorority members. She is living her passion through her business.

The seven Encore Leadership mindsets are very important to embrace as you confirm your passion. Gaining clarity around the intersection of the mindsets with your personal execution of your personal strategic plan is a means to assess the passion for your transformed life. Spend time shifting mindset habits to embrace your focus and desired level of passion. On a scale of 1-10, with 10 being high, rate the following about you:

1. Do you exemplify an attitude of gratitude?
2. Are you striving for Significance?
3. With whom are you sharing your wisdom?
4. Do you wake up every day to do work that matters?
5. Have you found a time and a place to escape for solitude?
6. What is the definition of your "Good Life"?
7. Do you honor and value your freedom to choose?

Dr. Richard Johnson suggests that a person can find her authentic work through the ReCareer process. (Johnson, 2009) He believes that his process will help you to discover and to pursue a purposeful work life that will stimulate your mind, fire your heart and feed your spirit. Complete the "ReCareer Assessment". Also, the "Hardy Personality Index" exercise is one of many tools that will continue to help you frame your Encore Leadership life that is designed as an outcome of the ReCareer process.

5. PROCLAIM VISION

The vision that you glorify in your mind, the Ideal that you enthrone in your heart – this you will build your life by, this you will become. – James Allen

What do you want to be doing 10 years from now? What will your world look like? What impact will you make? Who will be impacted by you?

John Maxwell (2001) offers a perspective for forming your vision with questions that help to shape your THINKing:

- **Look within You – What do you feel?** You can't borrow somebody else's vision. It must come from inside of you. The thing that brings it out is passion.

- **Look behind you – What have you learned?** Every leader's vision is based on his or her own personal experience. What does your past tell you about your future?

- **Look around you – What is happening to others?** As a leader, you must always take into account other people. If others aren't with you, you aren't leading.

- **Look ahead of you – What is the big picture?** Leaders don't get bogged down in the minutia. They see everything from the vantage point of the mountaintop. That's why their goals are called vision.

- **Look above you – What does God expect of you?** No vision is worthy of your life unless it fulfills your destiny, the purpose for which you were designed. You vision must contribute to your destiny.

- **Look beside you – What resources are available to you?** Your vision must be bigger than you. The greater it is, the more resources it will require. The best leaders bring all of the resources in their world into play to accomplish something great.

— Adapted from *Developing the Leader Within You*

Vision is a much debated and discussed subject as it relates to businesses and organizations. As an Encore Leader, it is critically important that one THINK about his personal vision with energy that mirrors a corporate strategic plan development so that it provides a pathway to a legacy that matters. In a simple context, Proverbs 29:18, the belief that without a vision, the people will perish resonates with many who are pursuing their life's work. (Felder, 2007)

Dr. Dorothy I. Height was a tremendous mentor and friend to me and to so many others, who were fortunate to have been in her presence. Her book, *Living with Purpose*, (2010) provides a wealth of insight to ponder as one really THINKs about leaving a legacy. In particular, her words for continued dialogue are applicable to Encore Leadership:

To move forward, we have to look at the world as it is becoming rather than how it has been. We have to see how to stretch ourselves to become more related to this ever-changing scenery. We have to gain a recognition not only that no one stands alone, but on a positive side, that we also need each other. (Height, 2010)

II. REDEFINE

Balance activity with serenity, wealth with simplicity, persistence with innovation, community with solitude, familiarity with adventure, constancy with change, leading with following. – Jonathan Lockwood Huie (2011)

The next phase of transforming your life is to REDEFINE what your Encore Leadership life will look like! There are three major steps that you should embrace to start this part of the process. They are:

6. **Design Personal Strategic Plan**

7. **Inventory Assets**

8. **Build Personal and Professional Network**

6. DESIGN PERSONAL STRATEGIC PLAN

Adaptability is a competency that should be renewed from your "first career." The ability to shift and embrace new directions in order to design your personal strategic plan is required. One must shift her THINKing of what the next phase of the transformed life will look like and consciously design a strategic plan to make it happen.

THINK about strategic plans that you have developed, worked on, driven or executed in other circles of your life. When were they successful? When did they not accomplish the mission that was set forth?

The exercises that are suggested in this phase mirror the approach to successfully developing and executing a strategic plan. Components of the strategic plan that we will focus on include:

1.   Vision
2.   Mission
3.   Objectives
4.   Goals

5. Strategies

6. Values

7. Measures of Success

PERSONAL STRATEGIC VISIONING
Name: Dates: 2___ - 2___

VISION					
MISSION					
OBJECTIVES	1. 2. 3. 4. 5.				
ST GOALS (2___)	1.	2.	3.	4.	5.
MT GOALS (2___ - 2___)	1	2	3	4	5
LT GOALS (2___ +)	1		2	3	4
STRATEGIES	1 2 3 4 5 6 7				
VALUES	1 2 3 4 5				
MEASURES	1 2 3 4 5				

Crystal Stairs, Inc.

©2009, Crystal Stairs, Inc.

Figure 18. Personal Strategic Visioning "Plan"

VISION

The vision for your personal strategic visioning plan should invoke a spirit of energy and enthusiasm that will sustain your daily adventures in your transformed life. Keep it simple and memorable. Create analogies and mantras that keep you focused and moving forward.

William James believed that *"human beings can alter their lives by altering their attitudes of mind."* (Nightingale, 1956) His additional statements supported his premise of attitude.

We need only in cold blood act as if the thing in question were real, and it will become infallibly real by growing into such a connection with our life that it will become real. It will become so knit with habit and emotion that our interests in it will be those which characterize belief... If you only care enough for a result you will almost certainly attain it. If you wish to be rich, you will be rich; if you wish to be learned, you will be learned; if you wish to be good, you will be good. Only you must, then, really wish these things, and wish them exclusively, and not wish at the same time a hundred other incompatible things just as strongly. (Nightingale, 1956)

Michael Beckwith authored a learning kit, *Life Visioning: A Step-by-Step Process for Realizing Your Highest Potential.* (2008) He encourages you to engage the process in order to "activate and refine your intuitive faculties so that you can have knowledge beyond the five senses, by seeing the invisible, and hearing the inaudible."

MISSION

Melissa Johnson provides a very profound mission statement that is an example for Encore Leaders to embrace.

I will live each moment with purpose divinely designed by God. I will walk with precision, be guided by principle and receive prosperity and favor in every facet of my life. I will live each new day with passion; there is no time for regret. I am a pioneer challenging the status quo, forging a new path with the seed I sow. Relentlessly, I pursue my purpose by touching and changing the lives of people everywhere I go. (Johnson, 2008, p. 41)

A mission statement provides a framework to communicate the work that one wants to engage in and make a difference. The mission is the intersection of passion and purpose that one envisions for his work.

OBJECTIVES

What will you achieve by driving your vision? What do you hope to achieve by executing your mission? These questions should further delineate the alignment of the personal strategic plan by generating specific goals to measure the objectives that are established.

GOALS

Setting goals is a very crucial and important component of transforming one's life. There is an abundance of literature that provides techniques and approaches. However, for this work, I opted to use the principles of goal setting shared by Gary Blair in his book, *Everything Counts!* (Blair, 2010) He first describes articulates that goal setting is a process. He shares the steps in the process as:

1.   Decisiveness
2.   Focus
3.   Actions
4.   Persistence
5.   Follow-through
6.   Victory.

In writing your goals, he offers six important questions to ask:

1.   What you specifically want to achieve?
2.   Why this achievement is so important?
3.   Who will help you achieve this goal?
4.   Where you stand in relation to this goal?
5.   How you plan on accomplishing this goal?
6.   When, on what date will you achieve your goal (pg 99)?

As a component of coaching, the document "10 Goals to Complete in the next 90 days" is the tool that is used in the coaching practice to document and drive toward accomplishment of goals. It is the backbone for coaching and for shifting to a transformed life. The goals should be SMART: specific, measurable, actionable, relevant and time-bound.

Establishing clarity by focusing on the timeline to achieve components of the personal strategic plan allows for the constant movement forward in accomplishing the plan. Establishing deadlines is a means to drive to a finish line. Constant movement of the finish line challenges the completion of the necessary work to accomplish the end game.

Jullien Gordon' book, *Good Excuse Goals: How to End Procrastination and Perfectionism Forever* (2009), has mastered a technique to achieve goals that entails specifics relative to purpose, people, and program. His approach to collaborating to achieve accountability and collaborative results is exercised with 30-day goal intervals and specific processes to drive toward the completion of the goals. This technique is used in the process to build networks of collaborative Encore Leaders and other individuals with various affinities for success.

In his book, *The 8 Cylinders of Success* (2009), Gordon outlines a goal setting technique that offers continued direction in setting SMART goals. With guiding questions and unique answers as examples, they include:

- Principles: What beliefs equate to success to me?
- Passions: What do I love doing and why?
- Problems: What social, scientific, technical, or personal problem do I want to solve?
- People: Who moves me to want to serve them and in what way?
- Positioning: What do I want to be #1 in the world at?
- Pioneers: Who are my models, mentors and guides?
- Picture: What's my vision for me and my world?
- Possibility: What's possible in the world with me that would not be possible without me?

Focusing on setting goals is a critical aspect of transforming the life of an Encore Leader. Whichever method results in winning the game is the one that should be embraced with vigor as one sets upon the Encore Leadership journey.

STRATEGIES

Connecting the dots from the vision to the measures of success is the end goal of strategy. How are you going to make it happen? What is the pathway to successfully executing the personal strategic plan? What are the unique linkages that through collaborative THINKing and doing can drive to even greater success your personal visioning plan?

VALUES

"Everything that's really worthwhile in life came to us free – our minds, our souls, our bodies, our hopes, our dreams, our ambitions, our intelligence, our love of family and children and friends and country." (Nightingale, 1956)

Establishing this provocative statement as a starting point for discussing values was a transformational moment for me. It allowed me to document the values that I believed in as I defined my personal strategic plan. Fundamentals ruled my compass of life, which were ingrained at a very early age by example and modeling the way. When I THINK about those values today, and hopefully those that have transferred to my family and friends, they would be easily observable and consistent in execution. Where I have fallen short of this mission to live my values, I take this moment to ask for forgiveness. However, they remain a constant companion of my journey.

1. Truth and Faith
2. Hard Work
3. Care for Others
4. To whom much has been given, one must give equally in return
5. It is more blessed to give than to receive
6. Education as a foundation to success

MEASURES OF SUCCESS

One of the toughest aspects of defining the personal strategic plan is to establish a definition of success that is measurable. Adopting a philosophy of quantifying success with your definition of success as the basis for the measure is an important action.

Lindbergh pondered how women could *remain whole in the midst of the distractions of life, how to remain balanced, no matter what centrifugal forces tend to pull one off center, how to remain strong, no matter what shocks come in at the periphery and tend to crack the nub of the wheel.* (Lindbergh, 1955, 1975, 1983, 2003) She answers the question with the thought of finding balance or an alternating rhythm between solitude and communion, between retreat and return. This is instructive as one seeks to shift from successful to significant — finding the alternating rhythm of the past and the future.

Booker T. Washington shared: *"I have learned that success is to be measured not so much by the position that one has reached in life as by the obstacles which he has had to overcome while trying to succeed."* Marian Wright Edelman utilizes *"The Measure of Our Success: A Letter to My Children and Yours"* (Edelman, 1992) to pass on her family legacy, her legacy of service and her twenty-five lessons for life.

Dr. Richard Johnson defined success as *"getting in touch with yourself, being your true self as fully as possible, and expressing your uniqueness in positive ways through your ReCareer. It means helping more people, clarifying your heart's desire, going after it, and achieving all this in a personal atmosphere of peace and benevolence."* (2009, p. 69)

What is your definition of success? How will you measure your success? Map the measures to the other components of the plan to ensure that your plan is aligned for successful execution. This accountability will also serve as a means to motivate and energize your efforts.

"Successful people don't avoid risks. They learn to manage them. They don't drive off cliffs into unexplored waters. They learn how deep the water is, and make sure there are no hidden obstacles. Then they plunge in." (Qubein, 1997, p. 83) Take the plunge and plan to transform your life!

Tracy offers the following guidance as "The Formula for High Productivity":

First, decide exactly what you want, in terms of your goals and objectives.

Second, make a list of everything that you have to do today to move you toward the achievement of those goals and objectives.

Third, organize your list by priority and select the most important single task you could complete right now.

Fourth, begin immediately on your number-one task and discipline yourself to work at it single-mindedly until it is 100 percent complete.

Finally, keep repeating, over and over to yourself, the wonderful words, "Do it now! Do it now! Do it now!" (Tracy, 2009, pp. 204-205)

Transform your life… define how you will measure your success as an Encore Leader, NOW!

7. INVENTORY ASSETS

Time, talent and treasure are valued assets for Encore Leaders. This step affords the opportunity to reassess the status of each of these elements. Often, travel has reminded me that we can better understand our gifts and allocate our time, talent and treasures by being observant of our environment.

While on vacation in Hawaii, there was a beautiful pond filled with koi fish. It was explained how the size that the fish would eventually grow to was dependent upon the size of the pond. The larger the pond, the larger the fish. As I observed the koi in the pond, it was evident that this open environment invited their growth into large and beautiful koi. I started to wonder how Encore Leaders constrain themselves by the environment that they create to swim in. The pond and the koi served as a reminder that we can create an environment of infinitesimal growth as long as we do not allow our environmental elements to confine our being.

TIME

"I can see time better – past and future – and can get in touch with the small speck I am and feel both the importance and the unimportance of my life." (Leider & Shapiro, 2012, p. 19)

The variable of time is an environmental element that must be wrestled with as individuals seek to transform themselves. Having and maintaining control of time is a huge task. While one may have dreamed of a traditional retirement, the definition changed along the journey of life, and the energy that we are accustomed to exerting did not magically turn off. When health issues set in as a result of allowing an environment to become stagnant and our movements less than energetic, we realize the risk of the gradual loss of energy.

If one shifts the THINKing of time to energy, as posited by Dr. Qubein, it opens the aperture of the innovative and creative, time and energy management by design. While managing through previous leadership roles of immense responsibility, time management techniques were adopted that enabled an enormous sense of accomplishment. Calendars, teams, assistants, perks for travel comfort... all such sorts of techniques facilitated the optimal use of time. Yet, with individual energy becoming a player in the day-to-day execution of tasks, time shifts to energy. Optimizing the energy in the space of time allocated to focus on the transformed life is a major shift in execution of asset utilization.

A pivotal question should be asked: "Is this activity worth my energy?" Dr. Kloser challenges people to focus on activities that contribute to the greatest value in your life and to do more of those. Do you know what those activities are? How do you gain clarity? She further offers to eliminate the activities that contribute little or no value to your life so that you reserve energy for the investment of energy necessary to pursue activities of value. She offers the following energy management tip:

You Have All the Time You Need

Breathe easy right now. In the divine scheme of things, you have absolutely all the time you need to fulfill your destiny and achieve all that you are meant to achieve in service to others. Rest in knowing it will all get done in divine right order and divine right time. (Kloser, 2012, p. 98)

Vicki Hitzges (2013) believes that one of the greatest time management lessons to learn is how to say NO. Her practical, yet profound approach to mastering this step of maintaining a positive mental attitude is to say NO with gratitude! In a nutshell, her advice is to thank the person for asking you to go, give or donate but stick with no. For example, "Thank you for asking me to the dance. It's gracious of you to ask. You always make me feel special. I'm sorry I can't." OR "Thank you for asking me to donate (to the cause. I don't give donations over the phone. But thank you for asking. Her formula, as you see, is to sincerely boost the ego of the other person but maintain a firm no.

TALENT

Understanding and targeting the current assets that one has acquired is the next major step of the transition journey. It is important to know what skills and talents should be leveraged as opposed to which should rest in the background. Think of this component of the process as providing a "self" report card.

Goodman (2008, p. 11) introduces a perspective with 389 ideas of reinventing retirement where she focuses on family, friends, health, what to do, and where to live. Emphasis on work, play, relationships, health, finances, and home environment provides food for a transitioning Encore Leader to consider as you transform to the Encore Leadership mindset. The ideas presented offer the opportunity to position your own THINKing relative to these subjects. This book generates concepts that can be further explored with a more formal assessment such as "Life Options®."

A focused approach to ascertaining the status of major components in life is the "Life Options® Assessment." This online tool accompanied by the book, *What Color is your Retirement*, (Johnson, 2006), offers a structured approach with questions and exercises that helps one ascertain his current readiness versus areas that need additional focus.

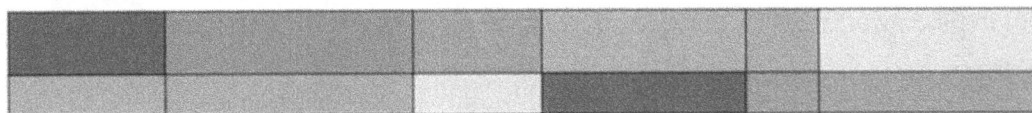

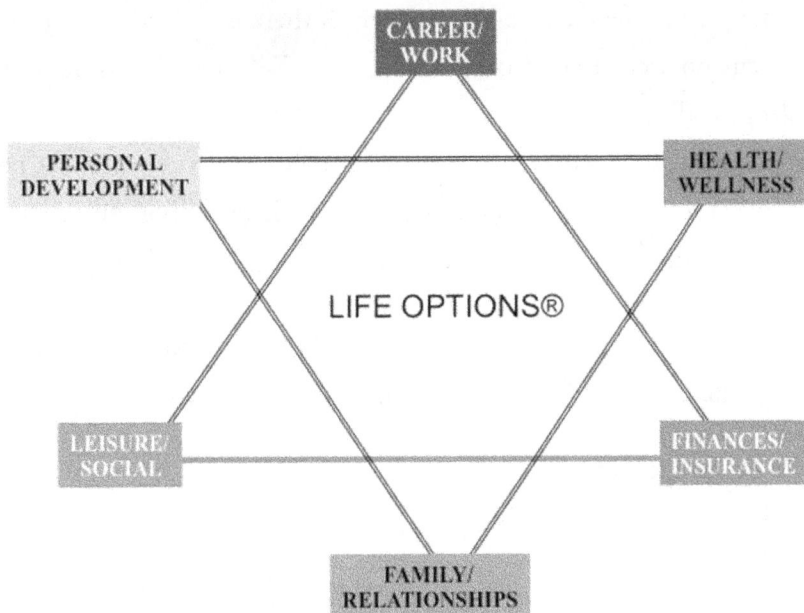

Life Options™ is a registered trademark of Retirement Options

Figure 19. Life Options® Assessment

This assessment provides insight through self assessment of where one currently resides as it relates to six focus areas:

1.   Career/Work
2.   Health/Wellness
3.   Finance/Insurance
4.   Family/Relationships
5.   Leisure/Social
6.   Personal Development

Taking a "time-out" to reflect and to prioritize areas of focus is a helpful exercise in strengthening future execution of your Encore Leadership life. Specific plans can be put in place, working with your coach, to make progress toward necessary shifts to move forward.

Coupled with an assessment of life options, if there is an interest in changing or continuing to focus on a career or work endeavor, the ReCareer Assessment and book (Johnson, 2009) provide a valuable process to analyze and work on specific areas related to a career opportunity. Understanding where one stands relative to changes needed to remain marketable and competitive is an important step in retooling the necessary skills to continue to successfully navigate an individual's career.

The ReCareer Assessment addresses the following areas under the clusters of Self-Assessment, Competencies, and Search Planning Skills:

1. ReCareer Identity
2. ReCareer Self Assessment
3. ReCareer Transition Hardiness
4. ReCareer Success Perception
5. ReCareer Goals and Decisions
6. ReCareer Calm and Confidence
7. ReCareer Maturation Vitality
8. ReCareer Aspirations
9. ReCareer Leisure-Life Competencies
10. ReCareer Positive Mental Attitude
11. ReCareer Search Planning Skills
12. ReCareer Resume and Cover Letter Writing Skills
13. ReCareer Search Time Management Skills
14. ReCareer Creative Interviewing Skills
15. ReCareer Assertive Communication Skills

Taking an inventory of your talents, skills, and gifts is a necessary component of the continued drive to transform your life. Leider and Shapiro ask the question, "Is your job your calling?" (2001, p. 53) The definition of job is certainly debatable, but in the context of what you wake up every day to do, is it your calling? Have you reinvented your life as a "marketable portfolio of talents" (Leider & Shapiro, 2012, p. 87) for whatever your chosen profession or community of engagement?

While I have personally taken, reviewed, and applied the Life Options® and the ReCareer Assessments, the benefit is reaped when focus on specific areas becomes the impetus for shifts that will lead you to greater influence and success as an Encore Leader.

TREASURE

Understanding the financial status of your life is a critical and often concerning inventory on which one must constantly focus. In many instances, giving and passing resources to the next generation is desired. Whatever your status, it is wise to take inventory of your financial well-being.

Legacy: Conversations About Wealth Transfer (Northern Trust, 2008, 2011) provides a framework for considering various fundamentals, strategies, planning for special assets, and creating a legacy. This book discusses the important subjects of understanding wealth transfer, having conversations, philanthropy, making gifts, lifetime giving strategies, asset management for various audiences, and a host of other key topics. These considerations should be inventoried as one specifically looks at the financial treasure component of the Encore Leadership life.

8. BUILD NETWORK

"In order to have the kinds of friendships and love relationships we dream of, we have to be the kind of friend and lover that other people dream of as well… Nutritious people are the people in our life who genuinely 'feed' our souls… those that love us with the fewest plans for our improvement, and that allow us to love them back completely." (Leider & Shapiro, 2012, pp. 60-61)

Our networks consist of individuals who enter our lives for various reasons. Some stay for a lifetime and others for various life events or seasons. Research reveals that people are "missing out on a sense of belonging to a group of people that share similar hopes and dreams or a sense of purpose in life." (Leider & Shapiro, 2012, p. 72) Thus, the creation of a network as you reinvigorate your life requires careful attention to your network of individuals who you choose to travel the transition stage of your journey.

First, let's understand what networking truly means. Often bantered around with senseless, mindless events, hopefully this step will provide insight as to the value and the true essence of the network.

Walker-Robertson penned a chapter in the book *The Power of Civility* and offers the definition of networking as

> people talking to each other sharing ideas, information and resources. Networking is what happens when there is a planned event or gathering with the primary goal of connecting with others. Networking is an action word with a fundamental focus on meeting people and having people meet you. It's what you do and how you do what you do to make people comfortable with and engaged by you. (Walker-Robertson, 2011, p. 95)

I share this definition as it resonates with the true essence of networking in action. As a master networker and student of social graces, Walker-Robertson is a walking case study of the skill of networking when mastered. Her elegance is both admirable and her results formidable because she makes networking work.

Walker-Robertson believes that "successful people possess highly-refined networking skills and a sense of civility in their interaction that is unmistakable." She describes "Influence" as observed through the reaction of others to the person with the positive shift of the room's ambiance. Walker-Robertson's ten tips provide a blueprint to refresh the skills of people who practice the skill and gives comfort to those individuals ready to tackle this critical element of building a network that works! The tips cover the subjects of:

1. Confirmation
2. Preparation
3. First Impressions
4. Introductions

5.   Remembering Names
6.   Conversation Skills
7.   Nonverbal Communication
8.   Business Card Protocol
9.   Following Up
10. Fielding Strangers

Harvard Business Review Online published an interesting article, "An Introvert's Guide to Networking." (Petrilli, 2012) This article offers three very provocative approaches to overcoming the fear of networking:

1.   Appreciate introversion rather than repudiate it;
2.   Stop being afraid to be the one to reach out;
3.   Prioritize to re-energize.

Overcome the fear of networking by utilizing these steps to take advantage of the opportunity to network to strengthen resources.

Now that we have introduced the importance of networking, let's explore critical aspects of building a network: Relationships, Influence, Team 100™, Trust, Endorsement and Connectedness.

RELATIONSHIPS

Relationships are the fundamental building blocks of networks. Curvie Burton depicts the interconnectedness of relationships and the distinctions in the Relationship Circles graphic (See Figure 20).

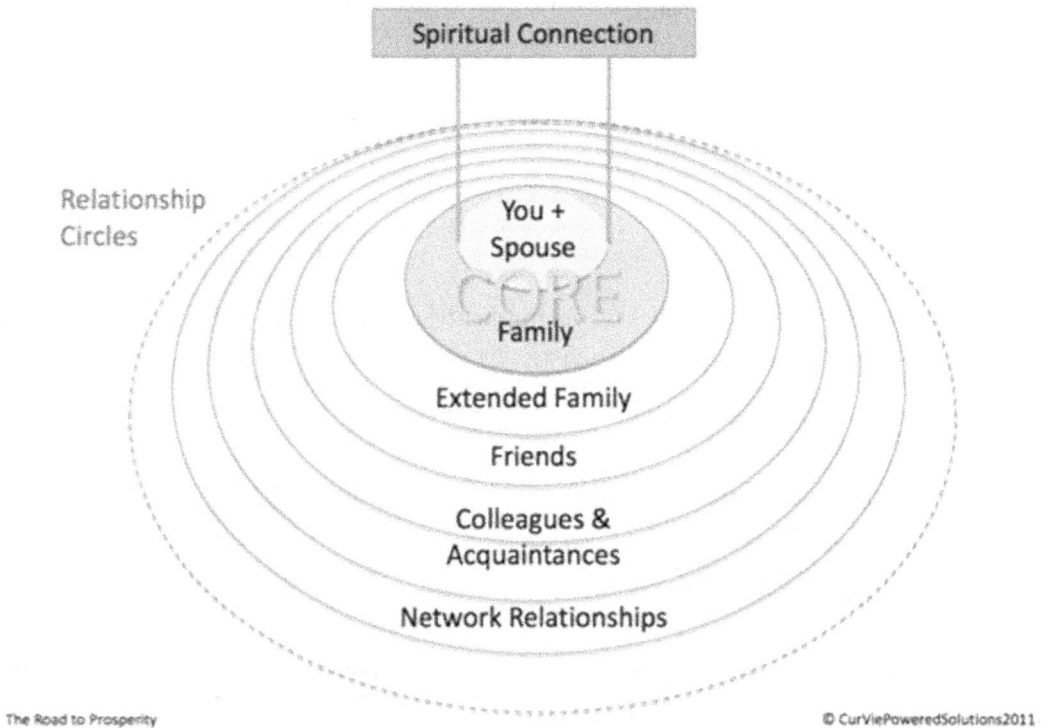

Figure 20. Relationship Circles

Career GPS (Bell, 2010) offers several keys to building successful relationships that should be engaged at any point in the leadership maturation life cycle. These keys are:

- Build relationships at all levels
- Get mentored
- Find a sponsor
- Design an elevator speech
- Cultivate allies
- Build a network
- Don't skip parties and social gatherings
- Give back

Leider and Shapiro offer an assessment of relationships intermingled with the critical element of listening. (2012, p. 144) This exercise provides an opportunity to map your current network of relationships with the quality of listening time that is exerted. Taking the time to review this exercise for key ties in your network will help define your Encore Leadership relationships.

I have been captive to the lessons provided by Terrie Williams since I met her and read her book, *The Personal Touch*. (1994) Her twenty tips to stand out among the crowd in building relationships are:

1. Know that your reputation is valuable;
2. Do what you say you're going to do;
3. Return all phone calls;
4. Treat everyone with respect and courtesy;
5. Be visible;
6. When you meet people, be mindful;
7. Try to develop a knack for remembering names;
8. Be an active listener;
9. Create a "small talk" notebook
10. Be sensitive to the "body language";
11. Send a follow-up note;
12. Get to know the support staff;
13. Know your profession;
14. Pass articles along with a note;
15. Keep a supply of greeting cards for all occasions;
16. Write... write... write.
17. Go through your Rolodex periodically;
18. Let people know that you are available to speak;
19. Selectively donate your services;
20. Remember what Mom used to tell you – say "thank you."

Assess where you are in terms of your skills in building relationships and jump-start this critical work.

INFLUENCE

The competencies that a Fortune 500 firm includes in its leadership training and development were validated as important by the participants who completed the transition survey. Influence was singled out as a key competency to acquire during the first career. Influence is defined as the skill of gaining support and commitment from others to mobilize for action. Influence is the ability to use internal and external contacts to forge relationships. It allows for a person to add spark and vigor to a work environment while gaining alignment.

The power of influence is a distinguishing factor in how well your network works. Distinct from appearing to know everyone and having everyone know you, consider how much influence you have in making things happen? Influence is earned and respected by invididuals who have mastered this skill.

What does your sphere of influence encompass? Take a look at your personal and professional network of friends, colleagues, family, and associates. Determine the strength of the various relationships. Assess the frequency of meaningful interaction. A common analogy for assessing the strength of network ties is to ask, "Is this relationship for a reason, a season, or for a lifetime?" Often, understanding the nuances of the response establishes the importance of the network tie and its strength.

TEAM 100™

Periodically documenting your network is a time consuming but rewarding endeavor. Completing the Team 100™ document is an excellent way to assess your team. Treat this process much like taking your car to the shop for a tune up or spring-cleaning your closet. Visualizing your team creates an opportunity to connect and re-connect with individuals who matter in your life.

These numerous network circles can be engaged in many ways at many different times. A conscious effort is required to nurture any relationship, in particular, the ones that you consider to be in your inner circle. The Team 100™ exercise may also reveal weak links or links that need to be strengthened. The book *212° the extra degree* (Parker, 2006) offers instructive provocation relative to owning the relationship, 100%. Instead of waiting for an invitation, extend the invitation. Instead of waiting for a call, make the call. Instead of waiting for an introduction, make the introduction.

Identifying and nurturing your Team 100™ is a great step toward building a network that matters, on purpose. See the *Encore Leadership Workbook* (at www.EncoreLeadership.com) for a framework to document your Team 100™.

TRUST

The element of greatest interest when discussing relationships is trust. Steven Covey's book, *The Speed of Trust*, provides an excellent approach for understanding and executing trusted relationships. (Covey, 2006) He offers the notion that "trust is the ultimate root and source of our influence."

As an Encore Leader, I find that trust is the one value that is a deal maker or a deal breaker. Either extreme can raise a flag of progress or retreat. Once trust is broken, it is difficult to repair. However, some relationships, when broken, are not meant to be repaired. Discerning the point of departure is a critical moment for Encore Leaders who are transforming their lives.

ENDORSEMENT

Endorsement is a tricky yet critical component of networking. Understanding the nuances associated with endorsement readies your network to receive or to be denied resources that are crucial to success. Suiter details the power of endorsement and the lack thereof in her book *The Ripple Effect* (2003). She notes five factors that impact gaining endorsement. They are:

1. Competence
   a. Technical
   b. Systems
   c. People
2. Communication Skills
   a. Oral
   b. Written
   c. Multimedia

3. Use of Feedback
    a. Asking for Feedback
    b. Receiving
    c. Processing
    d. Acting Upon
    e. Reporting Back
4. Appearance
    a. Eye Contact
    b. Body Language
    c. Manners
    d. Dress
5. Relative Position
    a. Title
    b. Location

In assessing your status of gaining endorsement from colleagues, associates and others, consider these principles of engagement:

1. Communicate in a consistent manner with sincere interest;
2. Stay connected especially when favors are not the purpose;
3. Keep confidential information private;
4. Carefully engage with social media relative to contacts and information sharing;
5. Differentiate between personal and professional relationships;
6. Utilize skills to support non-profit endeavors to share gifts and talents;
7. Write notes and share successes and recommendations with others;
8. Be open to feedback and offer feedback when requested or suggested;
9. Dress for the position to which you aspire or in a manner that establishes your brand;
10. Be known as a person beyond your company, title and position.

Pause for a moment and reflect on a few things that you should focus on to gain endorsements that matter at this stage of your encore leadership journey.

_____

_____

_____

_____

_____

_____

_____

CONNECTEDNESS

One should experience a sense of togetherness within her network. This is often described in terms of connectedness. How closely tied are you to various circles of family, friends, and acquaintances? Understanding the level of connectedness that exists versus the level desired is an exercise that warrants attention. The assessment of your network will allow you to allocate your time, talent and treasure in a more connected way to achieve your personal strategic vision.

Positively Impact Others

In every single moment that you spend with another person, you are impacting them one way or another. Ask yourself what kind of influence you WANT to have on other people Perhaps you want to be inspiring, motivating, healing, or accepting. Then take an honest assessment to see if the impact you want to make is aligned with how you are BEING with others. If not, don't judge yourself; simply choose to take a step in the direction of making a positive difference to others. (Kloser, 2012)

As an Encore Leader, keeping the sense of adventure, inspired by a supportive network, can be a game changer to motivate your Encore Leadership journey. Make sure your network gives you a strong sense of connectedness!

III. REINVEST

"Great breakthroughs result from a single moment in which a person lets go of their usual assumptions and looks at things from a new point of view."
– (Leider & Shapiro, 2012, p. 20)

Character and expression are key attributes in achieving a transformed life. Many people attempt to live by the notion that it is better to give than to receive.

The reinvention phases of re-examining and redefining lead to the opportunity to reinvest in an Encore Leader's transformation journey. There are two major focus areas to reinvest at this stage of transformation. They are:

9. Brand Identity

10. Execute

9. BRAND IDENTITY

"Some of the most critical components necessary for success in life are a strong sense of purpose, a passionate pursuit of that purpose, a clear vision and the capacity to develop your personal brand. Branding is the ability to refine and craft a uniqueness that becomes a mark of distinction which adds value to the brand." Dr. Myles Munroe (Johnson, 2008, p. 9)

One of the major adjustments that an Encore Leader has to embrace is the shift in identity. For so many years, life has been a consistent routine driven by the defined parameters of work and life. This step in the process invites the joy and freedom of exploring the many avenues of interest that have been suppressed while waiting for this moment in time. The daily grind of waking up and heading to the office disappears. Travel exhaustion is replaced with awakening to new adventures that are dictated by personal interest and not command performances. The Encore Leadership mindset of the freedom to choose kicks in!

Melissa Johnson defines brand as "the representation of your distinct and authentic value." She suggests clarity around knowing who you are, what you have to offer, and what makes you unique. Her steps to discern this insight requires you to:

1. Live Your Passion;
2. Understand Your Path;
3. Define the Problem;
4. Focus Your Position;
5. Work Your Plan;
6. Practice Partnerships and Networking;
7. Pass on the Legacy.

Key to note is Johnson's instruction that the reward of branding is to "package your gift to the world." (2008, p. 139)

Being known in your chosen space in a compelling and provocative manner is key to being able to communicate your transitioned self. This new branding should help you clarify to yourself and to others who you are and how you choose to invest your time, talent and treasure. Your passion and purpose should resonate with your brand identity. Determining your brand will serve as a personal guidepost for making decisions as to how you engage with others. Building an authentic and aggressive brand will serve to attract relationships that complement your transformation.

Ginny Clarke offers a framework for consideration in shaping your personal brand. (Clarke & Garrett, 2011) Her framework includes the following components and elements:

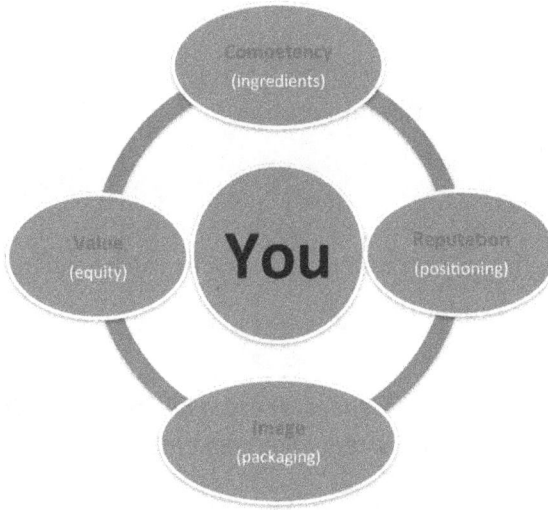

Figure 21. Clarke's Personal Brand

1. Competencies
   a. Skills
   b. Knowledge
   c. Capability
2. Reputation
   a. Credibility
   b. Capability
   c. Commitment
   d. Visibility
   e. Messaging
   f. Thought Leadership
   g. Humility
3. Image
   a. Appearance
   b. Speech
   c. Behavior
   d. Authenticity

4. Value
   a. Context
   b. Demand and Remuneration
   c. Value Proposition

Clarke's closing insight on branding is to affirm who you are. An example of her affirmation as an Encore Leader is:

"I am an expert and thought-leader on the subjects of organizational talent management and personal career management." (Clarke & Garrett, 2011)

I am a witness!

Coachable Moment: Helping to shape your authentic self requires stepping outside of your own hype and integrating the external hype of reality from different perspectives. What do others THINK? What have others observed? How do others see your contributions? How do others see your strengths and areas of focus? Gaining this perspective is often challenging for individuals who are not comfortable being vulnerable when they have been required for so long to be strong warriors. Encore Leaders in transition should be open to explore before determining their brand. Gaining clarity on intentions will help drive future value to those you serve. Alignment of your purpose and passion should resonate with your brand.

As I THINK about coaching conversations I have had with clients, I reflect on specific questions that I often ask clients about having others share with them their responses in order to gain an external point of view. They include:

1. What do you view my unique gift(s) to be that I do better than anyone else?
2. What is the initial impression I make on people?
3. What do people remember about me?
4. What stands out about me?
5. What am I doing when I am the happiest?

6.   What am I really good at doing?

7.   What conversations energize me?

8.   What work could I do 24x7 and enjoy?

9.   What gets me going off the deep end?

10.   Who do I remind you of?

11.   Describe me in one word.

12.   What should I THINK about changing to be more effective?

13.   Any other questions you THINK I should ask in order to gain greater insight about myself?

Optional question if you are brave enough to share your DiSC® behavior profile results…

14.   After reviewing my behavior assessment, I found two (or three) words that don't resonate. Can you shed some light on these words?

I asked my husband to share the answers to these questions with me at dinner one night, and it was very insightful. Of course, none of what he said was accurate, but it was insightful! End of story! Seriously, it's a great exercise for you to touch base with yourself.

David Samuel provides four phases for "Personal Branding Power" that can be instructive for branding during transition. (Samuel, 2006) These phases offer specific strategies to assist in planning, developing, branding, and connecting. Review the list in Appendix C and determine which actions are interesting to explore for you to focus on the components of your brand building as an Encore Leader.

Tom Peters penned the book, *The Brand You 50.* (Peters, 1999) This timeless masterpiece provides 50 provocative ways for you to transform yourself from an employee into a brand that shouts distinction, commitment, and passion. As a transitional exercise in branding, it is important to note that branding should occur in each stage of the leadership maturation life cycle. An interesting exercise that he shares as one of his techniques for branding is to complete the following:

1. Make a personal brand equity evaluation: What am I known for?
2. Develop a one-eighth or one-quarter size yellow pages ad for brand you/ me & Co. (Or in today's world, a Facebook or Twitter profile);
3. Create an eight-word personal positioning statement: Describe your position or work in eight words or less;
4. How about a bumper sticker that describes your essence? Ummm… THINKing!

Branding your Encore Leadership life is not an easy task. It will take multiple attempts to sing your song, but sing it you will!

SOCIAL MEDIA OPTIMIZATION

There are two fundamental steps to social media branding – establishing your Gravatar and your name. Gravatar (which means *Global Recognized Avatar*) is an image that will follow you from site to site every time you leave a comment on someone's blog post. It also gives instant brand recognition and the ability to link to your website and other personal information. What should your Gravatar be? Pam Perry, branding expert, suggests using the profile picture that you use on all your social media channels.

In determining your name for social media branding, decide whether to use your personal name, the business name, another name that is meaningful to your work, or create an entirely new name. **As a best practice rule, you want to ensure that the name you choose is consistent throughout all of your endeavors. To ensure consistency, once you choose a name, make sure it is available for use on various social media sites and domain name hosting.** Once the name is determined, you can then proceed with the next twelve branding steps for social media presence.

1. Purchase domain names that are closely aligned to your brand.
2. Set up your email address with your name and the domain name as the address (e.g., YourName@YourBrandURL.com). Route all email to one box (e.g., use Microsoft Outlook or Apple Mail to route Yahoo, Gmail, and YourBrandURL.com emails into one inbox).
3. Set up a Twitter account with your name.
4. Establish a Facebook presence with your name and a Facebook fan page. (Depending on your brand, you may want to keep your fan page and

personal page separate from each other. Doing so requires that you create your fan page while not logged into your personal page.)

5. Connect to others with a LinkedIn account that has your name.

6. Link together your social media accounts so that when you post on one site, it propagates to the other sites. (Most social media sites will allow you to connect most of your other social media pages. So you'll need to decide which social media account is the most flexible for what you want to do. Then, use that site to link all of your other accounts.)

7. Start a Pinterest account.

8. Integrate a photo app, like Photobucket.com or Flickr.com, or a video account, like YouTube, with your social media accounts. Photos and videos are excellent ways to add a rich dimension to your brand.

9. Develop a website that provides information regarding your branded business/endeavor. And before you start, you need to have a clear understanding of what you want your website to do. Will you sell products or services through your site? Will your site be informational only? Will you need to host your own videos or images gallery? Knowing the purpose for your site will save you tremendous time, effort, and money if and when you hire a website designer and programmer.

10. Start blogging at your branded blog site using a service like WordPress or Tumblr.

11. Launch a social media campaign that results in the purchase of your expert products and services. (When selling/promoting products or services through social media sites, make sure to abide by each site's rules and policies regarding these practices. Then, periodically review the terms of service to ensure that you are staying in compliance. Most sites will post notices of major changes, so watch out for these, too.)

12. Develop an ongoing social media education plan that forces you to adopt new tools into your platform. While this may seem, at first, to be a daunting undertaking, do know that social media tools and apps are becoming extremely easy to use. It's a simple matter of understanding how best to implement them to achieve the best outcomes.

These steps provide a high-level umbrella for a lot of work and understanding to accomplish and execute these suggestions. Given the rapid pace of change with social media, you should spend at least 5 hours every week educating yourself in some way on social media tools and trends. Also, include a technology "guru" in your network of resources. You will enjoy the ride, and your brand will stay fresh and exciting.

10. EXECUTE

"The journey of transformation starts from your core." – Ron Coquia

Performance is the single competency that did not shift from first career to second pursuits. Being results oriented and focused on accomplishing the tasks at hand in an exemplary manner has become a driving force as a normal modus operandi. Encore Leaders have a natural inclination to make things happen without regard to the journey when you are focused on the prize. Most Encore Leaders at some point have been the first, the best and the brightest, and/or, in the infamous talented tenth. The results of the executed performance has been heralded often in a matter of fact manner because the performance gets the job done.

Thus, we have reached the point of departure where readers of this book will emerge into one of two groups… those of you who are serious about defining your legacy, and those who are content just letting it happen. Individuals who are results oriented and performance driven understand that new adventures, outside of your comfort zone, are a welcome necessity for ongoing transformation. A graphic that I discovered on the internet recently caused pause for me, as I reflected on the execution step of the process.

Fearless   Excitement

Success   90% of the Population   Financial Freedom

Wealth   Mediocre Life   Just Survival   Dreams

Comfort Zone

Belief   Fear   Tired   Depression   Confidence

Settling   Average

Passion   What if I Can't   What if I CAN

Fulfillment   The Sky is the Limit

Figure 22. The Comfort Zone

Complacency rears its ugly head, unless one adopts the notion of living outside of life's comfort zone. While the pros and cons of being in and out of your natural self can be debated, this concept is a challenge for you to force yourself to ACT and to EXECUTE your plan. *The Strangest Secret* (Nightingale, 1956) reveals several truths that must be embraced:

1.   You will become what you think about;
2.   Remember the word "imagination" and let your mind begin to soar;
3.   Courageously concentrate on your goal every day;
4.   Save 10 percent of what you earn;
5.   Take action – ideas are worthless unless we act on them.

James Allen (1992) suggests that as a man thinketh in his heart so is he. I embraced this THINKing at a very early stage in my life and find it to be energizing to my journey. Having a constant destination in front of me, without being content when it's reached, has fueled my constant drive for new experiences and knowledge. This quest continues as I attempt to DO… REFLECT… THINK… BE… and ACT. This process keeps me energized and open to the unknown.

A guide and process that I find helpful in making decisions as I execute my plan was offered by Dr. Qubein. (1997, p. 83)

a. What is the best thing that could happen as a result of this action?
b. What is the worst that could happen as a result of this action?
c. What is the most likely result of this action?

IV. REIMAGINE

The microchip will colonize all rote activities. And we will have to scramble to reinvent ourselves – as we did when we came off the farm and went into the factory, and then as we were ejected from the factory and delivered to the white collar towers... The reinvented you and the reinvented me will have no choice but to scramble and add value in some meaningful way. – Tom Peters (2003)

THINK about the future. Reimagining your life is the final phase of the Encore Leadership process. This phase offers a time for reflection, a critical moment in the process of transformation. So many people are void of dreams. Without dreams, you cannot attract the life that you want. Encore Leadership is a lifelong, iterative process of learning and revising. It is important to carve out time to evaluate the journey and to innovate and reinvent whenever you reach a "transition tipping point."

The two major steps during this phase are:

11. **Evaluate the Journey**

12. **Innovate and Reinvent**

11. EVALUATE THE JOURNEY

As you take the time to reflect on your journey, are you able to *Whistle While You Work?* (Leider & Shapiro, 2001) This is a very appropriate question as you search to evaluate the transition journey. It is a question that offers the opportunity to respond positively and to continue along the path, or it provides the opportunity to reconsider the journey and to plot a new direction. What is your response?

Leider and Shapiro (2012, pp. 90-91) offer the following evaluation criteria of whether or not one is living a transformed life:

- *They have a purpose larger than their own needs, wants and desires – a sense of how their lives and work fit into the larger scheme of things.*

- *They have an internal compass which keeps them "truing" to their purpose in life.*
- *They have clear boundaries around their two most precious currencies – time and money.*
- *They have a sense of their potential talents, the limits of which have not been tested.*
- *They have marked adaptability when faced with obstacles – they simply handle them as a natural feature of living.*
- *Their abundant energy is infectious – it gives them and the people around them even more.*
- *They see their work as more than just a job; they are motivated by a sense of "calling."*
- *They have a feeling of lightness – a sense of not being burdened by the burdens they are carrying.*

On a scale of 1-10 (with 10 being the highest), how would you rate yourself against each of these measures?

12. INNOVATE AND REINVENT

What has amazed me most during my journey of transformation to Encore Leadership is the freedom to continually innovate and to explore new frontiers. The journey often includes new partners and new experiences. It keeps me fresh and excited about the next day. The journey wakes me up!

Leider and Shapiro noted that the major change from the first edition to the second edition of their book *Repacking* (2012, p. x) was the understanding that it requires ongoing reflection and choice. The journey required periodically unpacking, repacking, and several iterations. Very similar to Lewin's change theory in organization development of unfreezing, movement and refreezing, (Hatch, 2006, pp. 309-311) in order to adapt to constant change, one has to be able to transition through Bridges' transition stages of endings and the neutral zone in order to welcome new beginnings. (2004)

Bridges offers checklists in his book to manage the 3 phases of transition. (1999) These checklists provide the opportunity to assure Encore Leaders that they are navigating through the known phases of transition: the ending, the neutral zone, and the new beginning. It is instructive to review these checklists to maintain progression through the phases of transition.

Leider and Shapiro offer the following actions to reflect upon when repacking (2012):

1. Rediscover your hidden talents.
2. Reclaim your purpose.
3. Reinvent your job.
4. Reelect your personal board of directors.
5. Resharpen your growth edge.
6. Repack your relationship bags.
7. Reframe your time boundaries.
8. Rewrite your own vision of the good life.
9. Renew yourself daily.
10. Refind your smile.

I find these ten areas of reflection to be provocative as I continue to constantly transform the lives of Encore Leaders and my own life.

One of the means to innovate and reinvent is to periodically escape from the norms into the "wild." Strayed's account of how her journey exploring the Pacific Crest Trail renewed her being is an example of taking a sabbatical from a normal life. (Strayed, 2012) It is ironic that I discovered and read the book while on vacation in Hawaii, my 2012 respite from the daily drive of the world. Beautifully written, the book takes you to a place of understanding and desiring to escape to explore and renew.

How do you truly escape and renew?

Repacking, reinventing, rewiring and transforming life requires adopting a lifelong and proactive approach to the process. It is not a one-time event. THINK of it as changing grade levels in school. There is always something new to learn and a new adventure to explore. The Encore Leadership process energizes the journey of life.

Social psychologist Karl Weick "claimed that sensemaking is not based on discovering the truth about organizations, but on ordering our experiences so that our lives make sense." (Hatch, 2006, p. 44) He espouses that individuals form "maps and images as they look for order in their experiences; however, this order does not preexist their search." This theory gives insight to the need for experiences that inform the continuous process required to create an Encore Leadership life. Thus, the notion of a transformed life that is socially constructed through an ongoing series of experiences grounds the need for innovation and transformation.

Ron Coquia, a transitions and transformation coach, shares the belief that "with the right tools and support, transitions don't have to be so confusing. They can be an opportunity to transform yourself and your life into an expression of your passion and gift to the world."

PART III:

GETTING STARTED

GETTING STARTED

This section provides tips and pointers to start your journey of Encore Leadership. Establishing a coaching relationship, finding an accountability partner, and taking advantage of a myriad of resources are specific tasks that will jumpstart your transformation. Please review suggestions in the following pages to design a roadmap to move forward and also visit www.EncoreLeadership.com for additional information.

ENCORE LEADERSHIP COACHING

A person who is ready to tackle the tipping point that leads to Encore Leadership needs the assistance of a coach to move forward in an expeditious, yet cautious and calculated manner. Since I started my coaching practice in 2000, I have been coached by four certified coaches who offered me the support and accountability needed to make progress. It is with my own example and experience of having a coach and having coached others that I highly recommend that you make a coaching relationship a part of your transition journey to Encore Leadership.

The Visible Coaching Process© in Figure 23 has been adapted to work specifically with Encore Leaders. It is anchored with the Coachability Index, Selection of a Coach and Securing an Accountability Partner.

THE VISIBLE COACHING PROCESS©

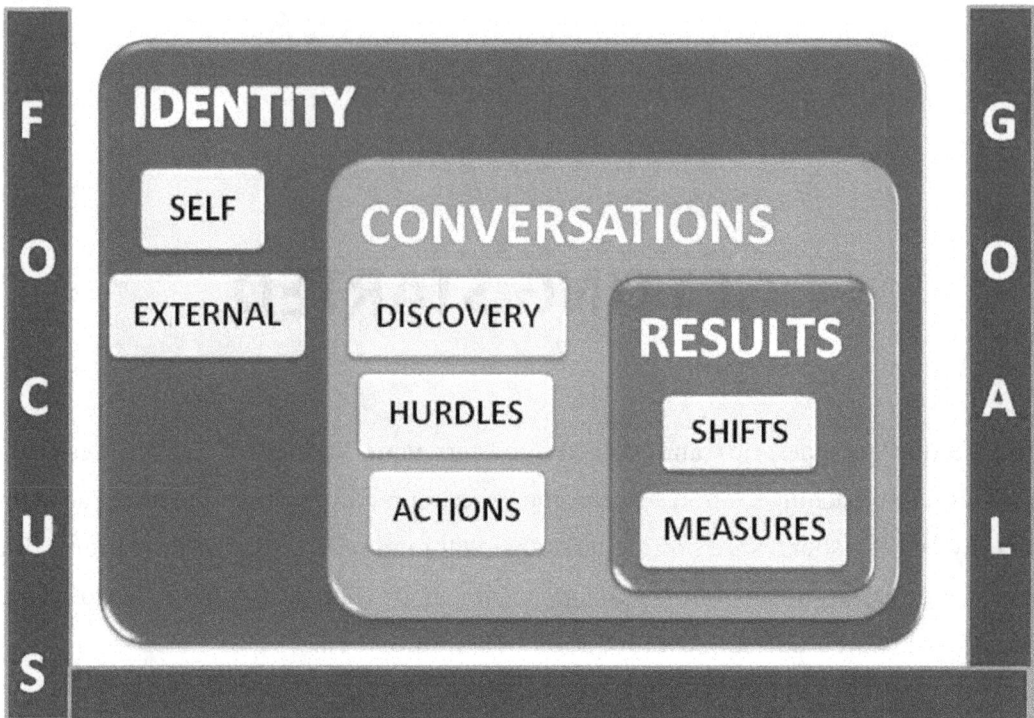

© 2009 Crystal Stairs, Inc.

Figure 23. The Visible Coaching Process©

COACHABILITY INDEX

The Coachability Index should be completed prior to deciding to invest in a coaching relationship. Individuals must be committed to the work required to successfully transition from their current state to their future state while resolving gaps in the transition process. The Coachability Index provides a quick assessment of your readiness. Review the Coachability Index in the *Encore Leadership Workbook* or at www.EncoreLeadership.com.

SELECTING A COACH

Visit www.EncoreLeadership.com to review profiles of coaches who have been certified to help other people transition to Encore Leadership. Interview two or three coaches so that you find a "fit" that results in the accountability that you will need to be successful. Understand their approach and process for coaching. Have the coaches provide a plan with specific actions to tackle your goals. Decide which style best "fits" your journey. Contract and get started.

ACCOUNTABILITY PARTNER

In addition to a professional coach, it is often beneficial to collaborate with another person whom you trust. This person should be not only a cheerleader for your success, but also a critique to keep you grounded on your journey. Consider the commonalities that may exist with your chosen partner, and also the tough love expected when in a valley. Establish a routine for courageous conversations and explorations. Make sure to establish a mutually beneficial, reciprocal relationship with your accountability partner.

RESOURCES

There are several methods of engagement that will help you get started on your Encore Leadership journey. They include:

- Encore Leadership Workbook
- Encore Leadership Dashboard
- Encore Leadership Journal
- Encore Leadership Assessments
- Encore Leadership Apps
- Encore Leadership Events
- Encore Leadership Seminars for Organizations
- Encore Leadership Target Audiences
- Encore Leadership Communities of Engagement
- Legacy Voices
- Stay Connected!

ENCORE LEADERSHIP WORKBOOK

Transformation is hard work. Thus, it is critical to be as focused as you have been on anything that is important to you as you seek to transform your life into building a legacy that matters. THINK of this as a project that is to be managed. Allocate time, find a quiet but thought-provocative space, bring your favorite beverage, and FOCUS on YOU!

The Encore Leadership Workbook will provide you with frameworks to THINK through each piece of your collage. Carefully complete the exercises and then reflect on the story through your work. What questions must you continue to ask? What answers are emerging? What caused you to be "stuck"? What did the "ah-ha moment" mean?

Take your time and THINK about the exercises and personalize the effort to architect your personal journey. Make sure you give the work your undivided attention and energy. Complete as many of the exercises as possible. Don't sell your transformed life short!

ENCORE LEADERSHIP DASHBOARD

One method to keep focused on the goal of transforming your life is to keep track of your progress. Use the Encore Leadership Dashboard to annotate your successful completion of each of the major exercises on the journey.

I remember when I was growing up that SRA readers were very exciting to me. I could follow my progress based on the color codes that I would mark on my master sheet. While working in the corporate world, I would track the progress of my team with a dashboard that included all the necessary key metrics. Thus, the genesis of my THINKing to use a dashboard as a means to record progress was a result of early experiences in life that informed my current work. It will be interesting to see what experiences inform your THINKing as you complete the work associated with your transformed life. Hopefully, you will set goals and reward yourself when you complete each exercise. Make it fun! Make it a daily habit! Make it the part of your day that you look forward to with excitement!

Use a set of color markers to add greater visibility to your dashboard. Find some unique stars decals or stickers that offer meaning to your achievements. Share your dashboard with your accountability partner or others who will help you to keep your eyes on the prize of the Encore Leadership life.

ENCORE LEADERSHIP DASHBOARD

PHASE	STEP	INSIGHT	DOCUMENTS	BLOG	STATUS	NOTES
TTP		Accountability Partner/Cohort EL Mindset TTP Questions	Transition Journey Dash Exercise Life Line Bucket List	O O O O	O	
RE-EXAMINE	1. Document Journey	EL Definition Testament	EL Assessment EL Executive Forum EL Coaching Plan/Goals EL Dashboard	O O O O	O	
	2. Determine Purpose	Strangest Secret Card	Life Purpose Worksheet Purpose Driven Life Work 10 Goals for EL	O O O	O	
	3. Explore Behavior Values Beliefs	DiSC Behavior Values Statement "I Believe in... " Statement	DiSC Report Values Report Personal Compass Trust Barometer Communities Template	O O O O O	O	
	4. Confirm Passion	Attitude Shifts Statement Passion Statement	Exercise Templates Passion Template Risk Analysis Template	O O O	O	
	5. Proclaim Vision	Vision Board Vision Statement	Transition Framework Life Visioning Work Pinterest	O O O	O	
REDEFINE	6. Design PSP Plan	Personal Strategic Plan (PSP)	Website Guide Solid Strategy Template	O O	O	
	7. Inventory Assets	Time, Talent ,and Treasure Map	Assessment Report Card Life Prospectus Document Financial Planning Notebook Legal Review Notebook Apple Classes Report	O O O O O	O	
	8. Build Network	Network SCOT Board of Advisors Sphere of Influence	Team 100, Love 25 Relationship Report Reason, Season, Lifetime Endorsement Exercise	O O O O	O	
REINVEST	9. Brand Identity	Brand ID Statement Brand Framework Elevator Speech Article/Chapter Book	Brand Development Event Branding Action Plan Marketing Collateral Social Media Plan	O O O O	O	
	10. EXECUTE	EL Dashboard Assessment Organized Event	Project Plan Barriers Organization Engagement Forum Attendance	O O O O	O	
REIMAGINE	11. Evaluate Plan	THINK Statement EL Journey Blog	EL Checkup Form EL SCOT EL Coaching Plan	O O O	O	
	12. Innovate and Reinvent	TTP Questions	TGIFiACT FELLOWS Invite EL Legacy Sessions Intellectual Stimulation Community Of Engagement	O O O O	O	
EL WORKBOOK			EL JOURNAL			

DATE: _____

Figure 24. Encore Leadership Dashboard

ENCORE LEADERSHIP JOURNAL

Journaling is tough duty. It is hard to take a few moments to capture the "ah-ha moments" of life. Yet, as your story unfolds, a journal will give you the fortitude and the strength to continue to build a tremendous legacy. As you write the history of your journey, the journal can take on whatever form you feel most comfortable with.

It could be a letter to your spouse, children, or another loved one.

It could be a daily proclamation of a special moment or memory.

You could clip visuals from news articles that remind you of the day.

You could use a photo from the past to capture and relive an experience.

Be creative. Make journaling a natural part of your day.

ENCORE LEADERSHIP ASSESSMENTS

Assessments provide unbiased and honest feedback about where you are on the journey. They invite the opportunity to hone time, talent and treasure to correlate to your Encore Leadership plan.

Use the Encore Leadership Assessments grid to further strengthen your skills to successfully complete the journey to transforming your life. The overall assessments are indicative of the various perspectives of insight that will provide you with a point of view for reflection and inflection.

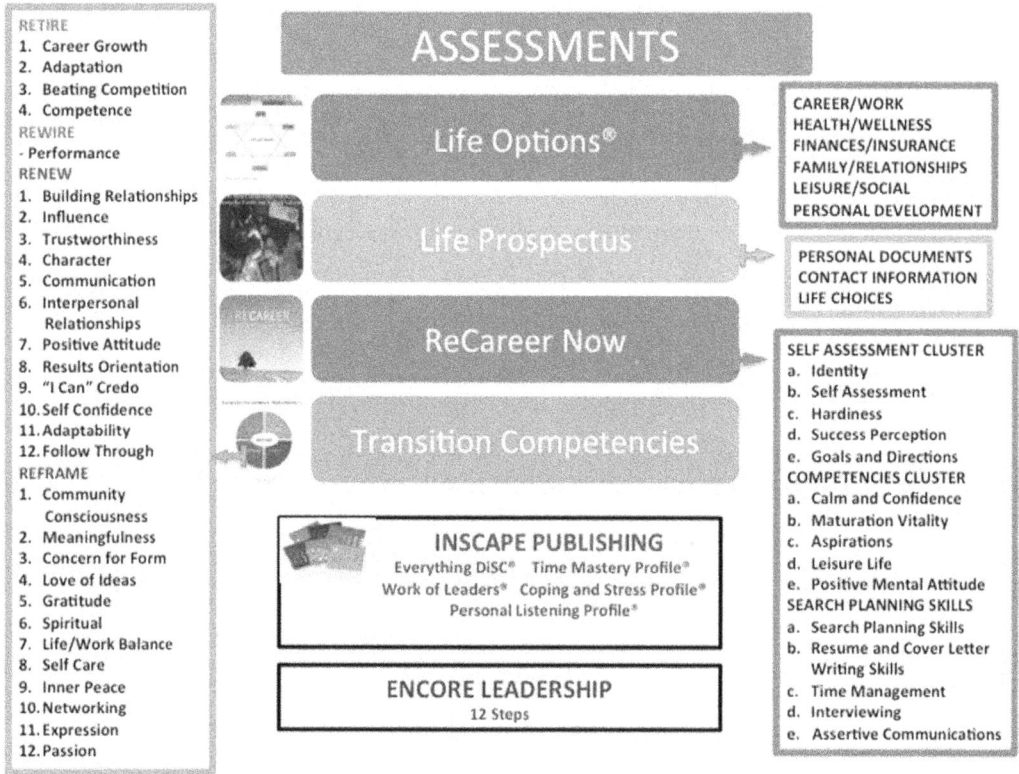

Figure 25. Encore Leadership Assessments and Transition Competencies

ENCORE LEADERSHIP APPS

- Encore Leadership Process Management
- Encore Leadership Relationships

Please visit www.EncoreLeadership.com for the latest developments on the project plan for the Encore Leadership Apps.

ENCORE LEADERSHIP EVENTS

The Encore Leadership Events sponsored and/or supported by Crystal Stairs, Inc. include:

Cohort Webinars
> Communities of Engagement
> Thought Leaders

Local and Regional Events
> Encore Leadership Cohorts
> Organization Partners

National Events
> National Forum
> Organization Partners

ENCORE LEADERSHIP SEMINARS FOR ORGANIZATIONS

If you are interested or are considering having your organization engage its Encore Leaders as a contributing membership category, please contact Crystal Stairs, Inc. for a strategic engagement review.

ENCORE LEADERSHIP TARGET AUDIENCES

This document provides a blueprint for various individuals and groups to collaborate and build communities of engagement. Crystal Stairs, Inc. will initially focus on Encore Leaders and Legacy Voices. However, transitions are encountered at various stages of the Leadership Maturation Life Cycle. Thus, the following audiences should consider Cracking the Transition Code and forming specific communities of engagement:

- Students transitioning into college or post-high school life;
- Aspiring Legacy Voices;
- Individuals moving into their first job;
- Individuals seeking professional promotional opportunities;
- People who are ready to find work that matters;

- Individuals interested in creating a legacy that matters;
- Organizations that understand the need to build a community through their legacy members.

ENCORE LEADERS COMMUNITIES OF ENGAGEMENT

Sign up to join other Encore Leaders, successful people committed to making a difference in their daily journey and leaving a legacy that matters. To join, register at www. EncoreLeadership.com. As you progress with engagement as an Encore Leader, expect to receive an invitation to join The Global Institute for Innovative and Collaborative THINKing (TGIFiACT). The designation of Encore Leader Coach and Encore Leader Fellow will be extended to those of you who truly set an example for others to follow and who meet the criteria for these designations.

Communities of engagement are forums and discussion groups where you can share interests, stories, and engagement opportunities. These communities are managed as social media groups with periodic events to convene conversations. The current communities are:

- Educator – Teaching others
- Education - Learning
- Education Advocacy – Impacting the education system
- Spiritual
- Philanthropy
- Foundation Leadership
- Foundation Creation
- Foundation Support
- Entrepreneur
- Coaching
- Author
- Publisher
- Family Historian
- Health

- Mentoring
- Golf
- Travel
- Other Personal Interests

Hitzges (2013) discussed that volunteering helps you to maintain a positive mental attitude. Her assessment of several studies pointed to the conclusions that volunteering makes you feel better, sharpen your mind, burn more calories and elongate your life. In particular, she highlights a study that suggests volunteers showed greater improvements in memory maintenance than individuals who did not volunteer.

Rath and Clifton offer research that revealed "Five Strategies for Increasing Positive Emotions." (Rath, 2004) Their findings:

1. Prevent Bucket Dipping
2. Shine a Light on What Is Right
3. Make Best Friends
4. Give Unexpectedly
5. Reverse the Golden Rule

Their book suggests that even the briefest interactions affect your longevity, health, productivity, and relationships. How full is your bucket?

Communities of engagement offer Encore Leaders the opportunity to connect with others to energize themselves while energizing others!

LEGACY VOICES

Legacy Voices are children, protégés and high-potential talent who are connected to Encore Leaders. Self nominated or nominated to participate in this community by Encore Leaders, Legacy Voices will evolve into a network of future leaders who are matriculating through various stages of the leadership maturation life cycle. This network will continue to develop, and announcements will be made as to its activities and events under the auspices of Encore Leaders within various communities of engagement.

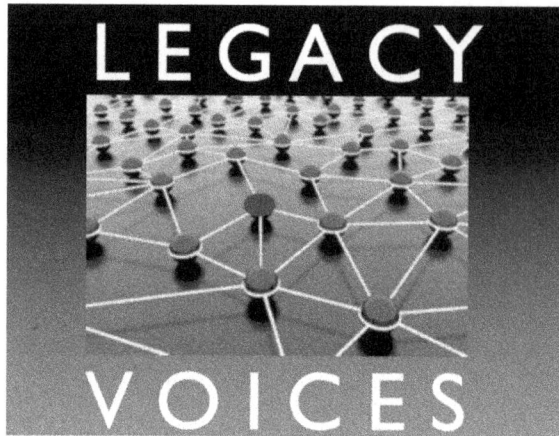

Figure 26. Legacy Voices

An amazing story of the power of the combination of an Encore Leader with a Legacy Voice is demonstrated by the book *How Great Women Lead: A Mother-Daughter Adventure Into the Lives of Women Shaping the World.* (St. John, 2012) When I first met Bonnie St. John, I was intrigued with her warmth and her passion for the work that resulted in her book. I ordered copies for many of the important women in my life. A few weeks later, she delivered them to me and signed each of them at an Executive Leadership Council meeting. As we chatted, I knew that I was in the presence of an Encore Leader who was doing work that mattered.

As I read the book, the inspirational legacy that she established with her daughter, Darcy Deane, will benefit young girls and women for centuries to come. The process, the results, the journey, and the amazing women who were profiled, truly is an example of the epitome of an Encore Leader and Legacy Voice experience. THANKS Bonnie and Darcy!

STAY CONNECTED...

To find out all the news and updates associated with Encore Leaders and Encore Leadership, sign up for our updates on various platforms. Our website, www. EncoreLeadership.com will be the central place for our static news, but we will aggressively embrace the immediacy of Twitter, Facebook, and other social media tools. We will evolve communication channels that will connect and engage like-minded transitioning individuals and organizations.

Blog and share your stories with Encore Leaders. Participate in an authored book with your expertise in a chapter. Support the books that will emerge from The Global Institute for Innovative and Collaborative THINKing (TGIFiACT). Share our stories with friends and associates, who will be energized to pursue or to step up their Encore Leadership life.

There are several specific objectives that the Institute will provide to support Encore Leaders. These include:

- Encourage the creation of environments for courageous conversations;
- Connect communities of engagement networks to leverage resources;
- Establish regional hubs and a national network of Encore Leaders;
- Publish stories to share wisdom;
- Build platforms to inspire entrepreneurship, angel investments, philanthropy and service endeavors;
- Partner with organizations exemplifying innovative engagement to solve issues impacting society;
- Extend the life cycle of membership in organizations through agendas that matter and attract Encore Leaders so they are available to reach back and give back to the organization;
- Establish profitable pursuits for Encore Leaders – financial, emotional, physical, spiritual and mattering.

Epilogue

It is almost midnight, but I still feel the energy flowing as I conclude *Encore Leadership: Transforming Time, Talent and Treasure into a Legacy that Matters!*

Adopting from the research that time is better viewed as energy, I hope that this book will inspire others to find passion around their work that fuels their energy for doing work that matters.

I continue to be a student of my work and appreciative to my clients, who allow me to travel their journey as I constantly change destinations on my own journey. The adventures that are now mile markers during my transformation mirror the stories told by others who have been fortunate to pursue Encore Leadership.

As I contemplate my next transition, I am committed to "connecting a community of countless Encore Leaders who count in countless ways." This is my passion. This is my mission.

Please step out on faith as you focus on transforming your life and enjoy the journey. While I may never step on the moon, I am blessed with dreams, aspirations, and a personal vision that keeps me seeking a higher purpose in life. I look forward to joining you in the communities of engagements and at events where our time, talent and treasure will be explored so that together we leave an invigorated legacy that truly matters!

DO IT... NOW!

Appendices

APPENDIX A: ENCORE LEADERSHIP GLOSSARY

TERM	YOUR ENCORE LEADERSHIP DEFINITION
Encore Leader	*Successful people who are engaged in legacy work that matters!*
Legacy Voice	*Children, protégés and high potential talent who are connected to Encore Leaders*
Change	*Movement to a different way of doing and/or being*
Transition	*The process of moving from one state that has ended to a future state that is envisioned*
Transformation	*Change, innovation and entrepreneurship infused into a process that is systematic, with purposeful and organized search for changes, systematic analysis, and the capacity to move resources from areas of lesser to greater productivity with a discipline of a predictable set of steps to become strategically aligned; Recognize need to change, create a new vision and institutionalize the change.* - Adapted from Tichy and Devanna, The Transformational Leader
Success	*"The progressive realization of a worthy ideal."* - Nightingale, The Strangest Secret
Significance/Significant	*The elevation of success to a spiritual meaningfulness that encompasses family and friends with a basis of faith.* - Adapted from Qubein, The Complete Blueprint for Personal and Professional Achievement
Vision	*How you seek to shape your world and influence others* *"Your vision is the promise of what you shall one day be."* - Allen, As A Man Thinketh, pg 43

TERM	YOUR ENCORE LEADERSHIP DEFINITION
Purpose	*What you believe you were put on this earth to do. Find your purpose, it fuels your fire, passion!*
Passion	*What sets us on fire!*
Behavior	*How you react and engage in a given situation and environment*
Values	*Those things that are non-negotiable in our life that guide our daily walk.* *Everything that's really worthwhile in life came to us free – our minds, our souls, our bodies, our hopes, our dreams, our ambitions, our intelligence, our love of family and children and friends and country.* - Nightingale, The Strangest Secret
Beliefs	*A view or perspective that you hold to be true*
Meaningfulness	*Having function or purpose, being highly focused and maintaining principles*
Mattering	*When one is consciously and intentionally living out beliefs that intersect with purpose which drives passion*

APPENDIX B: ONE PAGE JOURNAL

ENCORE LEADERSHIP ONE PAGE JOURNAL

PHASE	STEP	THINKing...
TRANSITION TIPPING POINT		
RE-EXAMINE	1. Document Journey	
	2. Determine Purpose	
	3. Explore Behavior Values Beliefs	
	4. Confirm Passion	
	5. Proclaim Vision	
REDEFINE	6. Design Personal Strategic Plan	
	7. Inventory Assets	
	8. Build Network	
REINVEST	9. Brand Identity	
	10. EXECUTE	
REIMAGINE	11. Evaluate Plan	
	12. Innovate and Reinvent	

©2012 Crystal Stairs, Inc.   DATE: _____

APPENDIX C: SAMUEL'S 65 PROVEN BRANDING STRATEGIES

PLANNING

1. Prepare a standard response to the question "What do you do?"
2. Perform a personal career SWOT analysis.
3. Keep current documentation of your career assets.
4. Assess your leadership profile (Myers-Briggs™ or DiSC®)
5. Envision and create a Personal Brand of value in the current business environment
6. Create a branding statement (Personal Value Statement – PVS) that describes your added value in 20-40 words.
7. Develop a list of the top five performance attributes valued by your company or organization.
8. Identify a Personal Brand role model and study him/her.
9. Write down the difference between your position and your purpose.
10. Note the three most important things to you in your professional roles.

DEVELOPING

11. Create an annual development plan with specific, measurable learning objectives.
12. Maintain a personal learning journal to document new knowledge or areas of expertise.
13. Identify the key gaps in your portfolio of career assets.
14. Become an "Agile Learner."
15. Develop knowledge or expertise in four new areas over the next twelve months.
16. Use PDF files to capture and store new learning.
17. Become an expert in the use of search engines.
18. Subscribe to an internet alert service like Google Alerts™ to keep current on new developments. (Use current technology subject matter alerts)
19. Solicit performance feedback from peers and protégés.
20. Establish a global mindset. (Extend/expand)
21. Develop several strong cultural relationship skills.
22. Enhance your collaboration skills.

23. Improve your information literacy.

24. Read one new book on development or leadership every month.

BRANDING

25. Position your Personal Value Statement (PVS) over as many branding channels as possible.

26. Write a one-page case study showcasing your expertise; one for each value claim in PVS.

    a. A challenge that you were faced with;

    b. What you did about it;

    c. Description of the results.

27. Create a narrative current bio. (Edit for audience)

28. Engage a photographer for a professional head shot for both hard copy and electronic use.

29. Draft a one-page Frequently Asked Questions (FAQs) sheet about your added value.

30. Produce a short PowerPoint presentation describing your Personal Value Statement.

31. Embed your Personal Value Statement into your standard email signature.

32. Develop an engaging and memorable outgoing voicemail message.

33. Generate two online profiles of yourself.

34. Develop a 'brag book' containing personal testimonials.

35. Keep a file of all performance appraisals or reviews.

36. Become the company thought leader for a specific strategically important niche topic.

37. Write a press release about your next public speaking opportunity.

38. Create a collection of internet links focused on your area of expertise to share with others.

39. Link your Personal Value Statement to the search engines.

40. Create a personal business card in addition to your company business card.

41. Develop a short annual report describing your growth and accomplishments during the preceding year.

42. Volunteer to facilitate your department's offsite planning meeting.

43. Deliver a presentation as a subject matter expert at an industry conference.

44. Be a presenter at a company sponsored meeting.

45. Establish personal advocate relationships strategically placed within the organization.

46. Get recognized in a project "success" announcement.

47. Develop a "vcard" with your Personal Value Statement embedded in the "Note" section.

48. Write a short 1,000-word article for publication.

49. Join a project team and continuously make meaningful contributions.

50. Join a committee at your house of worship or community center where you can contribute your expertise.

51. Speak about your professional role at your child's school.

52. Moderate a panel discussion at a professional conference.

53. Develop a personal web page.

54. Develop a blog to establish your expertise and stimulate dialogue with others about a particular topic. (Facebook fan page; Google)

55. Create personal marketing campaigns for each specific career transition.

56. Create a personal brochure describing your value.

57. Create a list of authored publications.

CONNECTING

58. Create a current database of your professional relationships.

59. Develop a mentoring relationship with one of your boss' peers.

60. Find three other emerging leaders to mentor.

61. Convene a personal advisory board.

62. Become an aggressive advocate for several professional peers.

63. Teach a how-to workshop on some professional topic.

64. Join a professional association and continuously make meaningful contributions.

65. Introduce a colleague to a new professional activity.

Bibliography

Allen, J. (1992). *As A Man Thinketh*. New York, NY: Barnes & Noble, Inc.

Arthur, M. (2007). *A Black Man Thinking: Raising Children* (Vol. 1). Oak Park, IL: A Black Man Thinking, LLC.

Beckwith, M. B. (2008). *Life Visioning: A Step-by-Step Process for Realizing Your Highest Potential*. Boulder, CO: Sounds True.

Bell Ph.D., E. L. (2010). *Career GPS: Strategies for Women Navigating the New Corporate Landscape*. New York, NY: HarperCollins Publishers.

Bell, E. E., & Nkomo, S. M. (2001). *OUR SEPARATE WAYS: Black and white women and the struggle for professional identity*. Boston, MA: Harvard Business School Press.

Bennis, W. (1993). *An Invented Life: Reflections on Leadership and Change*. Reading, MA: Addison-Wesley Publishing Company.

Blair, G. R. (2010). *Everything Counts! 52 Remarkable Ways to Inspire Excellence and Drive Results*. Hoboken, NJ: John Wiley & Sons.

Bourke, D. H. (2006). *Second Calling: Finding Passion & Purpose for the rest of your life*. Brentwood, TN: Integrity Publishers.

Bridges, W. (1999). *Managing Transitions: Making the Most of Change*. New York, NY: HarperCollins Publishers.

Bridges, W. (2004). *Transitions: Making Sense of Life's Changes; Strategies for coping with the difficult, painful, and confusing times in your life* (2nd Edition, 25th Anniversary Edition ed.). Cambridge, MA: Da Capo Press a Member of the Perseus Book Group.

Brokaw, T. (1998). *The Greatest Generation*. New York, NY: Random House.

Buford, B. (1994). *Half Time: Changing Your Game Plan from Success to Significance*. Grand Rapids, MI: Zondervan.

Buford, B. (2000). *Halftime: Changing Your Life Plan from Success to Significance.* Grand Rapids, MI: Zondervan.

Burton, M. L., & Wedemeyer, R. A. (1991). *In Transition: From the Harvard Business School Club of New York's Career Management Seminar.* New York, NY: HarperCollins Publishers.

Calkhoven, L. (2008). *Harriet Tubman: Leading the Way to Freedom.* New York, NY: Sterling Publishing Co., Inc.

Clarke, G., & Garrett, E. (2011). *Career Mapping: Charting Your Course in the New World of Work.* New York, NY: Morgan James Publishing.

Clinton, B. (2007). *Giving: How Each of Us Can Change the World.* New York, NY: Alfred A. Knopf.

Cobbs, P. (2005). *My American Life: From rage to entitlement.* New York, NY: Altria Books.

Coleman, H. (2006). *Empowering Yourself: The rules of the game* (Original Work Published 1996 ed.). Atlanta, GA: Coleman Publishing.

Covey, S. M. (2006). *The Speed of Trust: The One Thing That Changes Everything.* New York, NY: Simon & Schuster, Inc.

Daniels, C. (2005). Pioneers. *Fortune,* 152 (4), 72-88.

De Bono, E. (1970). *Lateral Thinking: Creativity Step by Step.* New York, NY: Harper Perennial.

De Bono, E. (1985). *Six Thinking Hats.* New York, NY: Back Bay Books.

De Bono, E. (2008). *Creativity Workout: 62 Exercises to Unlock Your Most Creative Ideas.* Berkeley, CA: Ulysses Press.

De Bono, E. (2009). *Think! Before It's Too Late.* London, England: Vermilion.

Douglass, F. (Original Work Published 1845). *Narrative of the life of Frederick Douglass, an American slave.* New York, NY: Anti Slavery Office and later Barnes & Noble Classics.

Edelman, M. W. (1992). *The Measure of Our Success: A Letter to My Children and Yours.* Boston, MA: Beacon Press.

Editors. (1997). Using Technology to Enhance Your Business. *Black Enterprise Magazine,* 27(9), 64-72.

Felder PhD, C. H. (Ed.). (2007). The Original African American Heritage Study Bible, King James Version. Valley Forge, PA: Judson Press.

Foster, J. (1998). Black Entrepreneurs and Corporate America. Speech presented at the Black Enterprise Entrepreneur's Luncheon sponsored by IBM, Orlando, FL.

Foster, J. M. (2009). Cracking the Transition Code: A Paradigmatic Framework of Competencies that Construct the Reality of 50+ Black Executive Transitions. *Dissertation, 267 (UMI No. 3367130)*.

Foster, J. M. (2002). *Due North! Strengthen Your Leadership Assets*. Hinsdale, IL: Crystal Stairs Publishers.

Frankl, V. (1963). *Man's Search for Meaning*. Pocket Books.

Gladwell, M. (2000). *The Tipping Point: How little things can make a big difference*. Boston, MA: Little, Brown and Company.

Goodly, T. W. (2007). Unfolding the Road Map to Success: A Grounded Theory Study of the Role of Agency and Structure in the Upward Mobility of African American Men. *Dissertation, 304. (UMI No. 3269580)*.

Goodman, M. (2008). *Reinventing Retirement: 389 Bright Ideas about Family, Friends, Health, What to Do, and Where to Live*. San Francisco, CA: Chronicle Books, LLC.

Gordon, J. (2009). *Good Excuse Goals: How to End Procrastination and Perfectionism Forever*. Brooklyn, NY: MVMT.

Gordon, J. (2009). *The 8 Cylinders of Success: How to align your personal and professional purpose*. Brooklyn, NY: MVMT.

Graves, E. (1996). Historical Connotation. *Black Enterprise Magazine*.

Graves, E. (1997). *How to Succeed in Business Without Being White*. New York, NY: HarperCollins.

Harrell, K. (2003). *An Attitude of Gratitude: 21 Life Lessons*. Carlsbad, CA: Hay House, Inc.

Harrell, K. (2004). *Attitude is Everything for Success: Say It, Believe It, Receive It*. Carsbad, CA: Hay House, Inc.

Harrell, K. (2000). *Attitude is Everything: 10 Life-Changing Steps to Turning Attitude into Action*. New York, NY: Cliff Street Books an Imprint of HarperCollins Publishers.

Hatch, M. J. (2006). *Organization Theory: Modern, symbolic and postmodern perspectives.* (A. L. Cunliffe, Ed.) New York, NY: Oxford Press.

Haven, C., & Ayotte, N. (Eds.). (2010). *The Little Black Book: Six-minute meditations on the Sunday Gospels of Lent (Cycle A).* Saginaw, MI: Little Books of the Diocese of Saginaw, Inc.

Height, D. I. (2010). *Living with Purpose: An Activist's Guide to Listening, Learning and Leading.* Washington, DC: The Dorothy I. Height Education Foundation.

Hitzges, V., *International Motivational Strategist and Best Selling Author.* (2013, September 26) Telephone Interview.

Hobson, A., & Clarke, J. (1997). *The Power of Passion: Achieve Your Own Everests.* Calgary, AB, Canada: Stewart Publishing.

Huie, J. L. (2011). *Quotes of Inspiration for Daily Inspiration – Daily Quote.* CreateSpace.

Hunter, N., & Chambers-Chima, D. (2005). *Choose to Lead: Advice, Tools, and Strategies for Women from Women.* Hilton Head, SC: Cameo Publications, LLC.

Isaacson, W. (2011). *Steve Jobs.* New York, NY: Simon and Schuster.

Jakes, T. D. (2002). *God's Leading Lady: Out of the Shadows and into the Light.* New York, NY: G. P. Putnam's Sons.

Johnson, M. D. (2008). *Brand Me*®. *Make Your Mark: Turn Passion into Profit.* Reynoldsburg, OH: Ambassador Press, LLC.

Johnson, PhD, R. (2006). *What color is your retirement? The LifeOptions® guidebook to discover, plan and live your retirement dream.* St. Louis, MO: Retirement Options.

Johnson, R. (2009). *ReCareer, find your authentic work: How to discover and pursue a purposeful ReCareer that stimulates your mind, fires your heart, and feeds your spirit.* St. Louis, MO: Richard P. Johnson.

Kimbro, D. (1998). *What Makes the Great Great: Strategies for Extraordinary Achievement.* New York, NY: Doubleday.

King James Version, The Holy Bible, Proverbs 29:18.

Kloser, C. (2012). *A Daily Dose of Love: Everyday Inspiration to Help You Remember What Your Heart Already Knows.* York, PA: Transformation Books.

Kloser, C. (2013). *Pebbles in the Pond: Transforming the World One Person at a Time* (Wave Two) York, PA: Transformation Books.

Leider, R. J., & Shapiro, D. A. (2012). *Repacking Your Bags: Lighten Your Load For the Good Life*. San Francisco, CA: Berrett-Koehler Publishers, Inc.

Leider, R. J. (2010). *The Power of Purpose: Find Meaning, Live Longer, Better*. San Francisco, CA: Berrett-Koehler Publishers, Inc.

Leider, R. J., & Shapiro, D. A. (2004). *Claiming your place at the fire: Living the second half of your life on purpose*. San Francisco, CA: Berrett-Koehler Publishers, Inc.

Leider, R. J., & Shapiro, D. A. (2001). *Whistle While You Work: Heeding Your Life's Calling*. San Francisco, CA: Berrett-Koehler Publishers, Inc.

Lindbergh, A. M. (1955, 1975, 1983, 2003). *Gift from the Sea*. New York, NY: Random House.

Loehr, J. (2007). *The Power of Story: Change your story, change your destiny in business and in life*. New York, NY: Simon & Schuster, Inc.

Losier, M. J. (2003, 2006). *Law of Attraction: The Science of Attracting More of What You Want and Less of What You Don't*. New York, NY: Wellness Central, Hatchette Book Group.

Martin, J. H. (2002, 2009). *Fulfilled: The Art and Joy of Balanced Living*. Chicago, IL: Nu Vision Media.

Maxwell, J. C. (2001). *The Right to Lead: A Study in Character and Courage*. Nashville, TN: J. Countryman®, a division of Thomas Nelson, Inc.

Maxwell, J. (2004). *Make Today Count: The Secret of Your Success is Determined by Your Daily Agenda*. New York, NY: Center Street, Hachette Book Group.

Maxwell, J. (2003). *Thinking for a Change: 11 Ways Highly Successful People Approach Life and Work*. New York, NY: Warner Books.

Mueller, R. K. (1978). *Career conflict: Management's inelegant dysfunction*. Lexington, MA: D. C. Heath and Company.

Neff, T., & Citrin, J. (1999). *Lessons from the Top: The Search for America's Best Business Leaders*. New York, NY: Doubleday.

Nightingale, E. (1956). *The Strangest Secret. Original Recording*. Wheeling, IL: Nightingale-Conant.

Northern Trust. (2008, 2011). *Legacy: Conversations About Wealth Transfer*. Deerfield Beach, FL: TriMark Press.

Novelli, B., & Workman, B. (2006). *50+: Igniting a revolution to reinvent America*. New York, NY: St. Martin's Press.

Obama, B. (2004). *Dreams from My Father: A Story of Race and Inheritance* (2nd ed.). New York, NY: Three Rivers Press. (Original work published 1995).

Obama, B. (2006). *The Audacity of Hope: Thoughts on Reclaiming the American Dream.* New York, NY: Random House.

Parker, S. & Anderson, M. (2006). *212° the extra degree.* Naperville, IL: Simple Truths, LLC.

Pausch, R. with Jeffrey Zaslow. (2008). *The Last Lecture.* New York, NY: Hyperion.

Peters, T. (2003). *Re-imagine! Business Excellence in a Disruptive Age.* (M. Slind, Ed.) London, England: Dorling Kindersley Limited.

Peters, T. (1999). *the brand you 50: Fifty ways to transform yourself from an "employee" into a brand that shouts distinction, commitment, and passion.* New York, NY: Alread A. Knoft.

Petrilli, L. (2012, January 12). *An Introvert's Guide to Networking.* Retrieved January 14, 2012, from Harvard Business Review: http:///www.lisapetrilli.com/the-introverts-guide/

Qubein, N. R. (1997). *Stairway to Success: The Complete Blueprint for Personal and Professional Achievement.* New York, NY: John Wiley & Sons.

Rath, T. & Clifton PhD, D. (2004). *How Full Is Your Bucket? Positive Strategies for Work and Life.* New York, NY: Gallup Press.

Russell-McCloud, P. (1999). *A Is for ATTITUDE: an alphabet for living.* New York, NY: HarperCollins Publishers, Inc.

Samuel, D. (2006). *Personal Branding Power: 65 Proven Strategies for Accelerated Career Growth.* Atlanta, GA: Lean Forward and Go!

Schultz, P. (2003). *1000 Places To See Before You Die: A Traveler's Life List.* New York, NY: Workman Publishing Company, Inc.

Shickler, S. & Waller, J. (2011). *The 7 Mindsets To Live Your Ultimate Life.* Roswell, GA: Ultimate Life Media a division of Excent Corporation.

St. John, B. & Deane, D. (2012). *How Great Women Lead: A Mother-Daughter Adventure Into the Lives of Women Shaping the World.* New York, NY: Hachette Book Group.

Statum, R. (2008). *Improving the Odds of Getting Beyond the Door.* Chicago, IL: Outskirts Press, Inc.

Stevens, A. (1994). *Jung.* New York, NY: Oxford University Press.

Storr, A. (1983). *The essential Jung.* Princeton, NJ: Princeton University Press.

Strayed, C. (2012). *Wild: From Lost to Found on the Pacific Crest Trail.* New York, NY: Alfred A. Knopf.

Suiter, J. (2003). *Energizing People: Unleashing the Power of DiSC.* Peachtree City, GA: Competitive Edge, Inc.

Suiter, J. (2003). *Exploring Values! Releasing the power of attitudes.* Peachtree City, GA: Competitive Edge, Inc.

Suiter, J. (2003). T*he Ripple Effect: How the Global Model of Endorsement Opens Doors to Success.* Peachtree City, GA: Competitive Edge, Inc.

Sykes, T. (2009). B. E. Titans. *Black Enterprise* (Online).

Tearte, J. M. (2013). *Encore Leadership Workbook: Doing Legacy Work That Matters!* Atlanta, GA: Crystal Stairs Publishers.

Tichy, N. M. (1986). *The Transformational Leader.* New York, NY: John Wiley & Sons.

Tracy, B. (2009). *Reinvention: How to Make the Rest of Your Life the Best of Your Life.* New York, NY: AMACOM.

Walker-Robertson, C. (2011). *Networking with Civility: The Ultimate Business Tool. The Power of Civility* (pp. 95-106). San Francisco, CA: Thrive Publishing.

Warren, R. (2002). *The Purpose Driven Life: What On Earth Am I Here For?* Grand Rapids, MI: Zondervan.

Washington, Booker T. (1901). *Up From Slavery: An Autobiography.* Garden City, NY: Doubleday.

Whaley, L. (2006). *Prisoners of Technology.* Bloomington, IN: Roof Top Publishing.

Whaley, L. (2004). *Reclaiming My Soul from the Lost and Found.* Bloomington, IN: First Books.

Williams, T. (1994). *The Personal Touch: What You Really Need to Succeed in Today's Fast Paced Business World.* New York, NY: Warner Books, Inc.

Index

A

Accomplish(ment)(s) v, xi, 21, 48, 55, 64, 65, 70, 93, 95, 98, 99, 103, 123, 153

Accountability 59, 99, 101, 133, 135, 137

Achieve(ing)(ment)(ments) xix, 4, 5, 8, 34, 49, 50, 54, 55, 74, 91, 97, 98, 99, 101, 115, 117, 119, 123, 137, 155, 158

ACT 61, 125, 126

Adapt(ability)(ed)(ing) xx, 12, 36, 44, 54, 58, 95, 128

Adjust(ing)(ment) 18, 88

Aesthetic 32, 81, 82, 83, 84, 86

Ah-ha moment(s) 136, 139

Align(ed)(ing)(ment) xx, 13, 59, 74, 77, 78, 79, 88, 97, 101, 112, 120, 122, 149, 157

Allen, James 54, 70, 71, 92, 126, 149, 155

Arthur, Maurice 8, 47, 155

Asset(s) xiii, 6, 79, 95, 102, 103, 104, 107, 152, 157

Attention 35, 58, 86, 90, 108, 115, 136

Attitude(s) 12, 36, 18, 45, 46, 47, 77, 80, 81, 82, 83, 87, 91, 92, 96, 104, 106, 143, 157, 158, 161

    Attitude of Gratitude 45, 46, 47, 77, 92, 157

    Mental 45, 46, 47, 91, 104, 106, 143

    Positive 12, 36, 46

Authentic(ity) 5, 49, 58, 59, 92, 118, 119, 120, 158

Ayotte, N. 158

B

Balance(ing)(s) 12, 31, 33, 42, 53, 58, 71, 73, 80, 95, 101

    See also Work, Work-life balance

BE 61, 126

Beckwith, Michael B. 97, 155

Behavior(al)(s) 44, 61, 64, 78, 79, 80, 82, 119, 121, 150

    Behavioral style(s) 78, 79, 80, 82,

Belief(s) 44, 50, 51, 78, 87, 88, 89, 93, 97, 99, 150

Believe(d)(ing)(s) xx, 6, 10, 11, 69, 74, 86, 89, 92, 96, 100, 102, 108, 150, 157

Bell, Dr. Ella vii, xiii, xxii, 110, 155

Bennis PhD, W. 155

Bible 157, 158

    See also Holy Bible;

    See also King James Holy Bible

Blair, Gary R. 98, 155

Blog(ging) 69, 122, 123, 145, 154

Bourke, Dale H. 89, 155

Brand(ed)(ing) xix, 40, 117, 118, 120, 121, 122, 123, 152, 153, 160

Brand identity 57, 117, 118

Bridges, W. 128, 129, 155

Brokaw, T. 6, 155

Brown, Angela 89, 90

Bucket list(s) 68, 69

Buford, Bob 42, 43, 49, 74, 155, 156

Burton, Curvie ix, 87, 109

Burton, M. L. 41, 156

C

Calkhoven, L. 156

Calm(ing) 34, 54, 67, 74, 84, 106

Career(s) xix, 4, 5, 6, 8, 9, 10, 11, 12, 13, 14, 16, 17, 18, 19, 21, 23, 36, 40, 41, 42, 69, 79, 80, 82, 85, 86, 95, 105, 106, 110, 112, 120, 124, 152, 154, 155, 156, 159, 160
See also Growth, Career;

See also First career

Challenge(d)(ing)(s) vii, xiii, xix, xxi, xxii, 6, 8, 18, 51, 53, 58, 67, 70, 83, 85, 97, 99, 103, 120, 125, 153

Chambers-Chima, D. 8, 158

Change(d)(ing)(s) xx, 3, 5, 8, 11, 15, 16, 17, 18, 21, 23, 42, 44, 46, 47, 49, 54, 58, 59, 66, 76, 78, 90, 94, 95, 97, 106, 103, 121, 123, 128, 130, 147, 149, 155, 156, 157, 159

Character 12, 36, 54, 71, 117, 159

Choice(s) xxii, 14, 24, 56, 57, 58, 77, 78, 102, 127, 128, 149, 160

Choose(ing) xxii, 45, 48, 50, 56, 57, 58, 73, 83, 92, 108, 117, 118, 122, 158

Citrin, J. 159

Clarity 30, 55, 56, 59, 64, 70, 92, 99, 103, 118, 120

Clarke, Ginny xviii, 41, 118, 119, 120, 156

Clarke, Jamie 91, 158

Clifton PhD, D. 143, 160

Clinton, Bill 47, 156

Coach(able)(ed)(es)(ing) 4, 7, 8, 59, 62, 79, 98, 106, 120, 130, 133, 134, 135, 142, 183, 184

Coachability Index 134

Cobbs M.D., Price 15, 156

Coincidence(s) xiii, 74, 90

Coleman, H. 156

Comfort zone 35, 124, 125
See also Zone

Commitment 6, 7, 22, 73, 112, 119, 121, 160

Communication 12, 36, 106, 109, 113, 145

Community(ies) xx, xxii, 5, 7, 12, 31, 42, 49, 56, 57, 58, 75, 79, 85, 90, 95, 107, 136, 141, 142, 143, 145, 147, 154, 183

Community consciousness 5, 12, 31, 79

Encore Leadership community(ies) 57, 136

Competence(ies)(y) xxii, 4, 5, 9, 10, 11, 12, 13, 14, 24, 25, 26, 27, 28, 30, 35, 36, 47, 57, 79, 89, 95, 106, 112, 119, 124, 140, 157 124, 183
See also Transition competencies

Competition 13, 36, 57, 79, 86

Beating 13, 36, 79, 86

Complacency 125

Confidence(ent) 12, 36, 47, 50, 90, 106
See also Self confidence

Connectedness 53, 58, 115, 116

Connecting 100, 108, 121

Control(ling) 21, 43, 45, 47, 54, 56, 70, 103

Coquia, Ron 124, 130

Covey, Steven M. 113, 156

Creativity 43, 73, 156

Credibility 119

Credo 12, 36

Crystal Stairs, Inc. iv, 40, 141, 183, 184

D

Daniels, C. 6, 156

Dass, Ram 76

Davis, Darwin ix, 6, 7

Deane, Darcy 144, 160

De Bono, E. 43, 44, 156

Desire(d)(ing)(s) xx, xxii, 5, 18, 19, 23, 32, 36, 51, 54, 58, 69, 83, 84, 86, 87, 90, 91, 92, 101, 107, 115, 127, 129, 159

Destination(s) 8, 47, 126, 147

Destiny 22, 43, 56, 93, 103, 159

Developed(ing)(ment)(ments) xx, xxii, 5, 8, 10, 11, 18, 20, 40, 75, 86, 87, 93, 95, 105, 112, 121, 128, 140, 152,153, 183

DiSC® 79, 121, 152

DO 61, 69, 147

Douglass, F. 156

E

Edelman, Marian Wright 101, 156

Education(al) xxi, 57, 77, 83, 100, 123, 142, 158, 183

Empowerment 73

Enable(s)(ling) 8, 50, 71, 183

Encore Leader(s) v, xi, xix, xx, xxi, xxii, 39, 40, 43, 44, 45, 46, 51, 54, 55, 57, 58, 59, 63, 65, 67, 70, 71, 75, 76, 77, 78, 83, 84, 85, 86, 87, 89, 93, 97, 99, 102, 104, 107, 113, 116, 117, 120, 121, 124, 129, 133, 141, 142, 144, 145, 147, 149, 183, 184

Encore Leadership v, xix, xx, xxii, 30, 35, 36, 39, 41, 44, 45, 47, 48, 56, 57, 61, 62, 63, 64, 70, 75, 77, 78, 79, 80, 82, 88, 89, 90, 91, 92, 93, 95, 99, 104, 105, 107, 111, 113, 116, 117, 122, 127, 128, 130, 133, 134, 136, 137, 138, 139, 140, 141, 145, 147, 149, 161, 183, 184

Endorsement 113, 161

Energize(d)(ing)(s) xxi, 46, 79, 101, 109, 121, 126, 130, 143, 145, 161

Engage(ment)(ments) xxi, xxii, 5, 6, 14, 15, 33, 35, 40, 46, 57, 58, 59, 62, 76, 79, 83, 84, 85, 86, 87, 91, 97, 107, 118, 136, 141, 142, 143, 145, 147, 150, 153, 183

Entrepreneur(ial)(s) xi, 8, 14, 23, 142, 157

Environment(al)(s) 5, 6, 17, 18, 30, 35, 42, 56, 58, 76, 77, 79, 102, 103, 104, 112, 145, 150, 152

Essence 56, 67, 69, 108, 122

EXECUTE 125

Execute(ing) iv, 40, 95, 97, 100, 113, 117, 123, 124, 126

Executive(s) vii, xxii, 4, 5, 6, 7, 8, 9, 10, 11, 13, 14, 46, 83, 85, 144, 157, 183

    Black 4, 5, 6, 7, 8, 9, 10, 11, 13

    Corporate 4, 5, 13

Experience(d)(ing)(s) iv, xx, xxi, 4, 7, 8, 20, 23, 32, 40, 43, 47, 48, 52, 53, 55, 56, 57, 61, 62, 64, 69, 73, 74, 77, 78, 79, 84, 85, 87, 93, 115, 119, 126, 128, 130, 133, 137, 139, 144, 184

Explore(ation)(ations)(d)(ing)(s) xiii, xix, xxii, 3, 4, 9, 10, 35, 39, 41, 43, 44, 45, 47, 55, 58, 64, 73, 74, 75, 78, 81, 82, 83, 84, 88, 104, 115, 116, 117, 120, 121, 128, 129, 130, 135, 147, 161,

Expression xxi, 13, 31, 32, 33, 59, 79, 83, 84, 117

F

Facebook xxi, 89, 122, 145, 154, 184

Failure 98

Faith 43, 47, 48, 49, 50, 89, 91, 147, 149

Family 7, 17, 40, 41, 42, 47, 48, 50, 51, 54, 68, 75, 87, 89, 90, 100, 101, 104, 105, 112, 114, 115, 142, 149, 150, 157, 183

Feedback 114, 139, 152

Felder PhD, C. H. 64, 93, 157

First career(s) 4, 5, 6, 8, 9, 10, 11, 12, 13, 14, 18, 23, 36, 80, 82, 85, 86, 95, 112, 124

Focus(ed)(ing) xix, xxii, 13, 18, 22, 28, 30, 32, 34, 35, 44, 46, 48, 55, 63, 65, 68, 69, 70, 71, 85, 86, 87, 88, 92, 95, 96, 98, 99, 103, 104, 105, 106, 107, 108, 117, 118, 120, 121, 124, 136, 137, 141, 147, 149, 150, 153, 183,

Follow through 12, 36

Forum(s) 67, 68, 141, 142

Foster PhD, J. M. xxii, 7, 71, 79, 82, 157

Framework(s) xxi, xxii, 4, 11, 13, 15, 16, 17, 75, 97, 107, 113, 118, 136, 157

Frankl, V. 58, 157

Freedom 20, 44, 45, 56, 57, 92, 117, 128, 156

G

Garrett, E. 41, 118, 120, 156

Give(ing)(s) xxi, 8, 21, 23, 33, 34, 35, 47, 49, 50, 51, 53, 54, 55, 56, 68, 70, 75, 77, 78, 85, 89, 90, 100, 107, 108, 110, 114, 116, 117, 122, 128, 130, 136, 139, 143, 145, 156

Gladwell, Malcomb 15, 157

Global Institute for Innovative and Collaborative THINKing, The 57, 70, 142, 145

Goal(s) 21, 41, 47, 48, 49, 69, 90, 91, 93, 95, 97, 98, 99, 100, 101, 103, 106, 108, 125, 126, 135, 137, 155, 157, 183

Golden Rule 143

Good life 45, 53, 55, 56, 59, 71, 92, 129, 158

Goodly PhD, T. W. vii, 157

Goodman, M. 104, 157

Gordon, Jullien 77, 78, 99, 157

Gratitude 12, 31, 33, 45, 46, 47, 77, 92, 104, 157

> *See also* Attitude of gratitude

Gravatar 122

Graves, Sr., Earl G. xi, 7, 8, 157

Growth 13, 32, 36, 79, 83, 84, 102, 129, 153, 160

> Career 13, 36, 79, 160

> Personal 32, 79, 83, 84

H

Happy(iness) 19, 47, 59, 83, 115

Harmony 34, 73, 83, 84

Harrell, Keith 45, 157

Hatch, M. J. 128, 130, 158

Haven, C. 158

Health(y) vii, 3, 19, 103, 104, 105, 115, 142, 143, 157

Height, Dorothy I. viii, 93, 94, 158

Hitzges, Vicki 47, 104, 143, 158

Hobson, Alan 91, 158

Holy Bible 158

> King James 157, 158

Holy Spirit 22, 89

Huie, Jonathan Lockwood 95, 158

Humility 119

Hunter, N. 8, 158

I

Identity v, 6, 57, 75, 106, 117, 118, 155

> *See also* Brand identity

Image(s) 119, 122, 123, 130

Individualistic 81, 82, 85, 86

Influence (d)(s) vii, 8, 12, 19, 36, 48, 52, 54, 68, 79, 107, 108, 112, 113, 149

Inner peace 12, 31, 34, 79

Innovate(ation)(ive) xix, xx, 5, 8, 45, 57, 70, 95, 103, 127, 128, 129, 130, 142, 145, 149, 183

Inspire(ation)(ational)(d)(ing)(s) v, vii, xxii, 5, 6, 41, 42, 44, 50, 52, 65, 73, 78, 91, 116, 144, 145, 147, 158,

Interconnectedness 88, 109

Introspection 64, 88

Isaacson, W. 83, 86, 158

J

Jakes, T. D. 52, 158

James, William 96

Jobs, Steve 83, 84, 86, 158

Johnson EdD, E. viii, 50, 158

Johnson, Melissa D. 57, 69, 91, 97, 117, 118, 158

Johnson, PhD, Richard 92, 101, 104, 106, 158

Journal(ing) xi, 73, 74, 136, 139, 139, 151, 152,

Journey v, vii, xiii, xx, xxi, 8, 43, 44, 45, 49, 55, 56, 57, 58, 59, 62, 63, 64, 65, 66, 67, 68, 69, 70, 76, 80, 82, 87, 91, 99, 100, 103, 104, 108, 116, 117, 124, 126, 127, 128, 129, 130, 133, 135, 136, 137, 139, 142, 144, 147, 184

> *See also* Encore Leadership journey;

> *See also* Transition journey

K

Kimbro PhD, D. 33, 158

King James Holy Bible 157, 158

King, Jr., Martin Luther xi, 35, 85

Kloser, Christine 71, 103, 115, 158

Knowledge xx, xxi, 5, 13, 21, 28, 31, 32, 33, 54, 69, 73, 76, 82, 97, 126, 152

L

Leader(s) v, xix, xx, xxi, xxii, 5, 20, 21, 41, 44, 46, 76, 77, 79, 87, 90, 93, 120, 141, 142, 143, 144, 145, 149, 153, 154, 159, 161, 183, 184

Leadership v, vii, viii, xiii, xix, xx, xxii, 6, 14, 18, 35, 39, 40, 41, 45, 47, 51, 57, 62, 63, 75, 79, 85, 87, 91, 103, 110, 112, 113, 119, 121, 133, 134, 136, 137, 138, 139, 140, 141, 142, 143, 144, 145, 147, 149, 152, 153, 155, 157, 161, 183, 184

> Leadership Maturation Life Cycle xix, 141

Learn(ed)(ing) 8, 18, 21, 32, 41, 43, 50, 54, 57, 66, 82, 83, 90, 93, 97, 101, 104, 127, 130, 142, 152, 158

Legacy i, iii, iv, xix, xx, xxii, 3, 5, 7, 15, 21, 41, 44, 45, 46, 50, 51, 52, 67, 69, 70, 74, 76, 77, 78, 93, 101, 107, 118, 124, 136, 139, 141, 142, 143, 144, 147, 149, 159, 161, 183

> Legacy Voice(s) 44, 76, 77, 78, 136, 141, 143, 144, 149

Legacy work xix, xxii, 7, 15, 41, 48, 76, 149, 161, 183

Leider, R. J. 33, 41, 49, 51, 52, 53, 55, 56, 58, 59, 71, 74, 75, 76, 78, 80, 102, 106, 107, 111, 117, 127, 128, 129, 158, 159

Life Compass® 80

Life cycle xix, xxii, 40, 47, 51, 75, 110, 121, 141, 143, 145, 183

Life Options® Assessment 104, 105

Lindbergh, Anne M. 53, 54, 100, 101, 159

Listen 49, 57, 58

Loehr, Jim 58, 159

Losier, M. J. 90, 159

M

Martin, Jacquie H. 73, 159

Mattering xx, 44, 45, 51, 52, 71, 77, 145, 150

Maxwell, John C. 46, 54, 92, 159

Meaningfulness 12, 31, 44, 150

Measures of success 96, 100

Media

> *See* Social media

Mentored(ing) 6, 7, 85, 110, 143, 154

Mentor(s) 6, 8, 42, 68, 87, 93, 99, 154

Microsoft Outlook 122

Mindset(s) 3, 45, 56, 73, 77, 92, 104, 117, 152, 160

Mission xx, 58, 91, 95, 97, 100

> Statement(s) 58, 97

Moore, W. Darin xxi

Motivate(d)(s) 5, 46, 81, 101, 116, 128

Mueller, R. K. xviii, 15, 16, 159

Munroe PhD, Myles 117

N

Neff, T. 159

Network(ing)(s) vii, viii, 4, 13, 20, 31, 34, 55, 57, 58, 95, 99, 107, 108, 109, 110, 111, 112, 113, 114, 115, 116, 118, 124, 143, 145, 160, 161, 183, 184

New skills 83

See also Skills

Nightingale, E. 47, 96, 97, 100, 125, 149, 150, 159

Nkomo PhD, S. M. xxii, 155

Northern Trust 107, 159

Novelli, William 3, 159

O

Obama, Barack 8, 159, 160

Objective(s) 11, 20, 23, 41, 64, 69, 76, 95, 97, 101, 145, 152

Objectivity 82

Opportunity(ies) viii, xi, xx, xxii, 3, 4, 6, 11, 17, 18, 20, 24, 28, 44, 46, 47, 53, 55, 56, 58, 64, 67, 68, 69, 77, 102, 104, 106, 109, 111, 112, 117, 127, 129, 139, 141, 142, 143, 153, 183

P

Parker, S. 112, 160

Passion(s) xix, xxi, 13, 18, 20, 28, 31, 35, 41, 44, 45, 46, 49, 64, 74, 75, 77, 84, 89, 91, 92, 93, 97, 99, 118, 120, 121, 130, 144, 147, 150, 155, 158, 160, 161

Pausch, Randy 50, 160

Peace 12, 31, 34, 43, 49, 74, 79, 89, 101

See also Inner peace

Pebbles in the Pond, Wave Two 73, 74, 158

Performance(s) 13, 18, 35, 79, 91, 117, 124, 152, 153

Perry, Pam 122

Personal growth 32, 79, 83, 84

See also Growth, Personal

Personal strategic vision 41, 104, 115

Peters, Tom 121, 127, 160

Petrilli, L. 109, 160

Philanthropy 107, 142, 145

Power 45, 52, 54, 58, 71, 73, 81, 86, 91, 108, 112, 113, 121, 144, 158, 159, 160, 161

Pray(er)(ers) 46, 89, 90

Principle(s) 32, 70, 73, 87, 97, 98, 99, 150

Problem solving 43, 59

Purpose(s) 23, 32, 35, 42, 43, 44, 46, 48, 50, 51, 55, 56, 57, 58, 64, 70, 71, 72, 73, 74, 75, 76, 77, 78, 85, 89, 91, 93, 97, 99, 107, 113, 115, 117, 118, 120, 123, 127, 128, 129, 147, 149, 150, 152, 155, 157, 158, 159, 161

Pursuit(s) xiii, 4, 5, 6, 7, 8, 9, 10, 11, 12, 13, 14, 23, 80, 82, 85, 86, 117, 124, 145

See also Second pursuit

Q

Qubein PhD, N. R. 48, 101, 103, 126, 149, 160

R

Rath, T. 143, 160

Receptive 45

Redefine(d)(ing)(s) 32, 47, 61, 117

Re-energize 109

Re-examination 64

Re-examine(ing) 61, 64, 117

REFLECT 61

Reflect(ed)(ing) xx, 50, 51, 52, 58, 61, 64, 65, 67, 75, 82, 89, 105, 120, 124, 127, 129, 136

Reframe(ing)(s) xx, 27, 30, 47, 129

Re-imagine(ing) 127, 160

Reinvent(ed)(ing) xix, 5, 30, 41, 43, 49, 61, 74, 104, 107, 127, 128, 129, 130, 157, 159

Reinvest 61, 117

Relationships 6, 10, 12, 17, 32, 34, 35, 36, 46, 49, 52, 56, 57, 68, 79, 83, 84, 104, 105, 107, 109, 110, 111, 112, 113, 114, 118, 129, 133, 134, 135, 140, 143, 152, 154

    Building 12, 36, 111

    Interpersonal 12, 36

    Relationship circles 34, 110

Renew(ed)(ing) 26, 36, 41, 64, 75, 95, 129

Repack(ing) 55, 57, 59, 128, 129, 130, 158

Reputation 111, 119

Respect(ed) iv, 7, 14, 20, 21, 67, 111, 112

Result(s) viii, 10, 11, 12, 17, 33, 36, 47, 54, 55, 58, 61, 79, 97, 99, 103, 117, 121, 123, 124, 135, 137, 144, 153, 183

    Results orientation 12

Retire(ment) 3, 4 5, 17, 18, 19, 21, 22, 26, 36, 41, 42, 103, 104, 157, 158

Reward(ing) 21, 98, 112, 118, 137

Rewire(ing) 27, 35, 130

Routine(ly) 49, 50, 117, 135

Russell-McCloud, Patricia 46, 160

S

Samuel, David 121, 152, 160

Schultz, P. 68, 160

Second pursuit(s) 4, 5, 6, 7, 8, 10, 11, 12, 13, 14, 23, 80, 82, 85, 86, 124

Self 4, 12, 31, 34, 36, 41, 42, 46, 54, 56, 64, 70, 78, 79, 84, 87, 101, 104, 105, 106, 115, 118, 120, 125, 143

    Assessment 64, 105, 106

    Awareness 46

    Care 12, 31, 34, 79

    Confidence 12, 36

Shapiro, D. A. 33, 41, 49, 51, 52, 53, 55, 56, 57, 58, 59, 71, 74, 75, 76, 78, 80, 102, 106, 107, 111, 117, 127, 128, 129, 158, 159

Share(d)(ing)(s) xi, xiii, xxi, 4, 6, 7, 8, 13, 22, 23, 33, 35, 43, 45, 46, 47, 49, 50, 52, 55, 58, 67, 68, 69, 70, 73, 76, 77, 84, 86, 91, 92, 101, 102, 107, 108, 115, 120, 121, 137, 142, 145, 153, 184

Shickler, S. 77, 160

Shift(ed)(ing)(s) xix, xx, 3, 4, 14, 17, 30, 34, 35, 40, 41, 43, 59, 78, 79, 82, 84, 85, 86, 87, 92, 95, 98, 101, 103, 106, 107, 108, 117, 124, 183

Significance(ant) xix, 4, 5, 6, 7, 8, 10, 12, 13, 17, 44, 45, 47, 48, 49, 63, 70, 82, 87, 92, 101, 102, 149, 155, 156, 160, 183

Silence 53

Skills 17, 28, 32, 36, 41, 42, 47, 48, 54, 55, 58, 79, 82, 83, 104, 106, 108, 109, 111, 112, 113, 139, 152

    New 83

SMART 98, 99

Social media 58, 122, 123, 124, 142, 145

Solitude v, 32, 45, 53, 59, 92, 95, 101

Solving

    See Problem solving

Speech 110, 119, 157

Spiritual(ity) 12, 22, 31, 33, 48, 53, 54, 70, 73, 88, 89, 142, 145, 149

Sponsor(ed)(s) 6, 17, 19, 68, 85, 110, 141, 154, 157

Statement, vision

    See Vision, Vision statements

Statum, R. 8, 160

Stevens, A. 160

St. John, Bonnie 144, 160

Storr, A. 160

Story(ies) xi, xx, xxi, 4, 5, 6, 7, 8, 41, 53, 58, 59, 65, 67, 68, 75, 84, 87, 121, 136, 139, 142, 144, 145, 147, 159

Storytellers 59

Strategic 41, 48, 55, 92, 93, 95, 96, 97, 99, 100, 104, 115, 141, 183

Strategy(ies) 48, 96, 100, 107, 100, 121, 143, 152, 155, 158, 160

Strayed, C. 129, 160

Success(ful) viii, xi, xix, xx, 4, 5, 6, 8, 9, 11, 12, 21, 23, 28, 35, 43, 44, 45, 47, 48, 49, 54, 55, 56, 57, 62, 63, 64, 65, 68, 70, 71, 73, 77, 79, 83, 95, 96, 98, 99, 100, 101, 102, 106, 107, 108, 110, 113, 117, 135, 137, 142, 149, 154, 155, 156, 157, 159, 160, 161, 183

Successful to significant xix, 48, 63, 70, 101

See also Measures of success

Suiter, Judy 78, 79, 81, 83, 84, 86, 113, 161

Support(ed)(ing)(ive)(s) ix, xxi, 7, 41, 46, 58, 83, 85, 86, 87, 90, 96, 111, 112, 116, 133, 141, 142, 145

Sykes, T. 7, 161

T

Talent(ed)(s) i, iii, iv, v, xx, 3, 4, 5, 7, 8, 15, 23, 33, 41, 48, 54, 56, 69, 76, 102, 104, 106, 107, 115, 118, 120, 124, 128, 129, 139, 143, 147, 149, 183

Teach(ing) 20, 21, 22, 85, 89, 142, 154

Team 100™ 112, 113

Tearte PhD, Jylla 91, 161, 183, 184

Technology 19, 23, 53, 58, 67, 124, 152, 156, 161

Testimony 89

TGIFiACT 57, 58, 70, 145.

See also Global Institute for Innovative and Collaborative THINKing, The

Thankful(ness) 33, 47

The Global Institute for Innovative and Collaborative THINKing

See TGIFiACT

THINK(ing)(s) v, vii, viii, xix, xxi, 5, 8, 15, 30, 33, 34, 35, 42, 44, 45, 46, 48, 53, 54, 55, 57, 59, 61, 64, 65, 66, 69, 70, 77, 82, 87, 90, 92, 93, 95, 100, 102, 103, 104, 120, 122, 126, 127, 130, 136, 137, 142, 145

Tichy, N. M. xx, 149, 161

Time i, iii, iv, ix, xix, xx, xxi, 3, 7, 8, 10, 11, 15, 18, 19, 21, 23, 24, 32, 41, 42, 43, 47, 48, 49, 50, 51, 52, 53, 54, 56, 57, 59, 64, 65, 66, 67, 68, 69, 70, 75, 76, 77, 78, 79, 80, 83, 88, 90, 92, 97, 98, 102, 103, 104, 105, 106, 111, 112, 115, 117, 118, 122, 123, 127, 128, 129, 130, 136, 139, 147, 155, 183

Management 103, 104, 106

Tipping point(s) 5, 15, 16, 17, 39, 41, 44, 50, 56, 61, 62, 127, 133, 157

See also Transition tipping point

Tracy, Brian 69, 101, 161

Tradition(al)(s) 5, 41, 77, 81, 82, 86, 87, 103

Traits 79, 82, 85

Transform(ation)(ed)(ing) i, iii, iv, xix, xx, xxi, 4, 15, 17, 21, 39, 44, 46, 57, 58, 62, 64, 65, 70, 78, 82, 84, 85, 92, 95, 96, 98, 99, 101, 102, 103, 104, 106, 113, 117, 118, 121, 124, 127, 128, 129, 130, 133, 136, 137, 139, 147, 149, 160

Transition(al)(ed)(ing)(s) xiii, xiii, xix, xxii, 4, 5, 6, 8, 9, 10, 11, 12, 13, 14, 16, 17, 18, 23, 24, 25, 28, 30, 41, 42, 43, 44, 47, 56, 57, 58, 59, 6 61, 65, 6, 69, 79, 80, 82, 85, 86, 87, 104, 106, 108, 112, 118, 120, 121, 127, 128, 129, 130, 133, 134, 140, 141, 145, 149, 154, 155, 156, 157, 183

Competency(ies) 4, 5, 9, 10, 11, 12, 24, 25, 28, 30, 47, 140

Journey xiii, 8, 56, 65, 66, 69, 104, 127, 133

Transition tipping point(s) 5, 16, 17, 43, 44, 56, 61, 127

Treasure(s) i, iii, iv, xx, 15, 41, 56, 102, 104, 107, 115, 118, 139, 147, 183

Trust(ed) 22, 35, 49, 57, 107, 113, 135, 156, 159

Truth(s) 19, 20, 23, 54, 67, 100, 125, 130, 155, 156, 158, 159, 160, 161

Twitter 122, 145

U

Utilitarian 81, 82, 83, 85, 86

V

Values 22, 31, 32, 42, 43, 44, 50, 64, 78, 80, 81, 82, 84, 85, 86, 87, 88, 96, 100, 150, 161

Value proposition 120

Vision xx, 22, 30, 41, 44, 48, 56, 58, 64, 71, 92, 93, 95, 96, 97, 99, 100, 104, 115, 117, 129, 147, 149, 159

Vision statements 58

See also Personal strategic vision

Volunteer(ing)(s) 31, 41, 85, 143, 153

W

Walker-Robertson, Cheryl viii, 108, 161

Waller, J. 160

Warren, Rick 73, 161

Washington, Booker T. 101, 161

Wealth 83, 93, 95, 107, 159

Wedemeyer, R. A. 41, 156

Weick, Karl 130

Whaley, L. 8, 53, 161

Williams, Terrie viii, 111, 161

Wisdom 4, 8, 45, 49, 50, 54, 76, 92, 116, 145

Witness 120

Womack, Carter D. viii, 70

Work iv, v, vii, viii, xix, xx, xxi, xxii, 7, 8, 12, 14, 15, 17, 18, 19, 21, 22, 23, 31, 33, 41, 42, 45, 46, 51, 52, 53, 55, 56, 57, 59, 64, 65, 68, 70, 74, 76, 77, 83, 85, 86, 91, 92, 93, 97, 98, 99, 100, 102, 104, 105, 106, 111, 112, 117, 118, 121, 122, 123, 127, 128, 134, 136, 137, 141, 144, 147, 149, 156, 158, 159, 160, 161, 183, 184

Work-life balance 53

See also Legacy work

Wylie, Greg ix, 46

Y

YouTube 123, 184

Z

Zaslow, Jeffrey 50, 160

Zone 35, 124, 125, 128, 129

About The Author

Jylla Moore Tearte, Ph.D.

Mother, Wife, Transitions Scholar Practitioner, Executive Coach, Consultant, Strategic Facilitator, Author, Publisher and Former Corporate Executive

Jylla Moore Tearte, PhD was one of IBM's top women executives with more than 20 years of various leadership assignments that spanned the globe. A nationally acclaimed Encore Leader, she is the President and CEO of Crystal Stairs, Inc. and is recognized for her innovative and insightful work with individuals who have been successful and seek to contribute legacy work to society. As COO for Tearte Associates, Jylla manages the Tearte Family Foundation, a portfolio of education partnerships that provide scholarships and grants to designated organizations for their scholars. She has authored several books and processes that enable clients to optimize their time, talent and treasure through collaborative networks of community engagement opportunities and resources. She lives in Atlanta, Georgia with her husband, Curtis.

ABOUT CRYSTAL STAIRS, INC.

Crystal Stairs, Inc. exists to build a network of transformative leaders by coaching pivotal transitions of the leadership maturation life cycle with a core competency of Encore Leaders. The firm offers innovative services focused on talent development and creating legacies that matter. Services include: Encore Leadership and Executive Coaching; assessments; training; consulting and strategic visioning for individuals, corporations, educational institutions, government entities and organizations. Founded in 2000, clients attest to becoming more results-driven, goal oriented, and shifting from success to significant.

For further information, please visit:

www.Crystal-Stairs.com

You can also contact us at:

Crystal Stairs, Inc., P. O Box 12215, Atlanta, GA 30355 USA

Email: Info@Crystal-Stairs.com

We invite you to share your experiences with Encore Leadership. If you find unique information or techniques to extend best practices within this book, please share it. If you have suggestions for additional information to include in this document, please let us know. Together our work will guarantee that this will be an incredible journey. THANKS in advance for your contributions.

Dr. Jylla Moore Tearte, CEO
Crystal Stairs, Inc.

Please visit us to join our network discussions or to request information on the following services:

- Workshops and Seminars (Face to face and Webinars)
- Become a best selling book author by contributing to an Encore Leader Chapter Book
- Encore Leadership Coaching
- Assessments

Join the Encore Leadership Movement

www.EncoreLeadership.com

www.Twitter.com/DrJylla
#EncoreLeader

www.Facebook.com/EncoreLeadership

www.Pinterest.com/EncoreLeaders/

www.YouTube.com/DrJylla

Crystal Stairs, Inc., P.O. Box 12215, Atlanta, GA 30355

DrJylla@EncoreLeadership.com

Special Credits and Thanks

Marketing – Eight:31 LLC • Photographer – Justin Scott Parr
Graphics – The Onyx Collection Media Group
Page Layout & eBook Conversions – the Ink Studio

Notes:

Notes:

Notes:

Notes:

Notes:

Notes:

Notes:

www.ingramcontent.com/pod-product-compliance
Lightning Source LLC
Chambersburg PA
CBHW081415270326
41931CB00015B/3280